£ 4·99　　　19-5-92

501
WAYS TO
SAVE MONEY

PAMELA DONALD

D0263471

PIATKUS

Other books by Pamela Donald
published by Piatkus

1001 Supersavers
501 DIY Supersavers
501 Gardening Tips

Acknowledgements

Thank you to everyone who helped me
put all this together. Often the people
most anxious to assist are also unduly
modest about being singled out for
special thanks. But Donna Waywell and
Beverley Ireson at British Telecom,
Ashley Holmes of The Consumers'
Association, Geoff Dossetter of the
Retail Motor Industry Federation, and
'Just John' – a man who can at the AA
– should know that they are much
appreciated.

Copyright © Pamela Donald 1992

First published in 1992 by
Judy Piatkus (Publishers) Limited,
5 Windmill Street, London W1P 1HF

**The moral right of the author
has been asserted**

*A catalogue record for this book is available
from the British Library*

ISBN 0-7499-1135-2

Cover design and illustration by Ken Leeder
Cartoons by Ron McTrusty
Set in Linotron Times by
Computerset Ltd, Harmondsworth, Middlesex
Printed and bound in Great Britain by
Mackays of Chatham plc

Contents

Introduction

Needless to say this book was inspired by the latest recession. However, the 501 suggestions for saving money will also help you to do your bit for the environment by resourcefully making the best of what you have and not cluttering your life with waste.

This is not a tramp's manual. I too have been poor and rich and back to poor at times in my life, and I agree with whoever it was who said that 'Rich is better'. There is nothing agreeable or virtuous about being seriously hard up, unless you're a nun perhaps. On the positive side, we are in a buyer's market and it has never been more fashionable to live frugally.

Why is the Princess of Wales anxious to reveal that she lets down the hems on the young princes' trousers rather than donate them to the Sandringham annual jumble sale? And why does her mother in law allow it to be known that she is a staunch supporter of the energy saving movement, switching off lights the second they are no longer needed?

It's not because they are afraid of the electricity bills or of causing offence to the servants by offering them cast-off school uniforms. Rather it's because there is something enormously satisfying about being thrifty as opposed to being mean.

Playing the miser can be a soul destroying and lonely business, and you don't have to go to depressing and time-consuming lengths to economise, as you will see from the tips in this book. What is important is to give yourself occasional treats out of the money you'll save by adopting these 501 suggestions for living better on less.

Pamela Donald

Money and Legal Matters

Organising Your Finances

<u>1</u> Where finances are concerned, it really will reward you to be well organised. Start a filing system with whatever your space and funds will allow – it could be a secondhand filing cabinet or a cheap concertina cardboard folder. Use it to store important receipts, guarantees and other documents, plus a list of renewal dates to jog your memory about car tax and servicing, insurance policy premiums, etc. There could be costly penalties if you let these lapse.

<u>2</u> Draw up a monthly balance sheet of income versus expenditure and then you will be able to instigate cutbacks in spending as necessary, rather than getting into debt. This sounds obvious but is a simple strategy that is often ignored until debts get out of hand.

3 If you are having problems balancing income with expenditure, find out just where your money goes by keeping a record. Enter in a notebook every single item of expenditure, however small, from postage stamps to unexpected repairs on the car or washing machine. Do this over a two month period to see where big cuts in spending can be made. Then, after cutting out all the frills, if you still can't see a way to balance your accounts get hold of a copy of *Which Benefit* (booklet number FB2) from your local CAB (Citizens Advice Bureau), post office or DSS office. This will tell you if you are eligible for financial assistance.

4 It is far easier to keep tabs on your finances with a monthly bank statement rather than waiting three or six months between statements. It shouldn't cost any more either, but do check this when you inform your bank you would like to receive monthly statements from now on.

5 If you are in serious financial difficulties, never delay in contacting the people to whom you are in debt. Offer to pay at least something towards the debt now and try to arrange to pay affordable instalments for the balance. The CAB gives excellent advice on overdue payments to credit companies, mortgage lenders, etc. You may be able to reduce your monthly payments and pay back the loan over a greater length of time. But sort out any debt problems as quickly as possible before matters are taken to court, or you will end up paying even more in costs.

6   Companies to which you pay regular bills for service – telephone, gas, electricity etc, offer budget schemes whereby you spread the cost and pay the anticipated amounts in instalments over the year. The only snag is that you may be paying out more than necessary, especially if you are intending to make economies from now on. However, at the end of the budget year you will be credited if you have overpaid. You may prefer to work out your own budget scheme, based on the anticipated total of next year's household bills. Use last year's bills as a guide, and include a generous allowance for inflation. Divide this total by 12 to find the amount you should pay into your own budget account each month to enable you to settle bills as they are due.

7   It's worth checking that you're not still paying standing orders or direct debits for goods and services you no longer use or need. Make a note of when renewals are due, and give plenty of warning in writing if you wish to cancel a subscription or annual charge paid by one of these methods. Many companies rely on your forgetfulness to cancel such payments.

Banks and Building Societies

8   Always check each item on a bank or credit card statement before filing it away or paying it and query any unexpected interest charge, unauthorised debit or double payment immediately.

9   If your current account tends always to be in credit, make sure that your bank or building society is giving you interest on it. The rate will be lower than that paid to deposit accounts but it will be worth having. Don't assume that just because your bank introduces an interest paying current account you will automatically be transferred to it.

10 If you have a substantial amount of money that isn't needed for the next few weeks, hold it in your deposit account but give instructions to your bank for an automatic transfer to be made to your current account when the latter falls below a certain level. This way you will get maximum interest on the money without risking overdraft charges.

11 Many of the national newspapers, such as *The Daily Telegraph* on Saturday, keep you up to date with best interest rates on offer for different types of account, or read *Blay's Money-master,* published each month and available at local libraries.

12 Find out how much the hidden extras levied as bank charges can take from your account – even when you are in credit. Paying credit card dues or the bills for gas and electricity over the counter can carry a couple of pounds service charge depending on the bank. A banker's draft for larger items, such as buying a car, can cost considerably more.

13 If writing a cheque for an unavoidable item will make you overdrawn, and you don't have an overdraft facility, it may pay you to use your credit card instead, if possible. Even if you can't pay the whole balance off when it appears on the next statement, the interest you will be charged probably won't be as much as bank charges for an unauthorised overdraft. Check with your bank what the penalties are and compare them to the credit card company's interest rate.

○ *Students*

14 The major source of finance for students comes from the high street banks who perform a ritual courtship each autumn, offering potential account holders record and clothes vouchers, interest-free overdrafts, etc. Study the market and open more than one account with the minimum amount required to get the maximum amount of freebies.

15   Consider your options with charitable trusts who make funds
available to students. Read *Money for Study* from Family
Welfare Enterprises, 501-505 Kingsland Road, London E8
4AU. Telephone: 071-254 6251.

See also 23, 425, 428, 429, 466 and 295.

Credit Cards

16   Credit cards cost you nothing if you shop around for a card
with no annual charge, and always settle your account in full
each month by the due date, so avoiding hefty interest
charges. The two important dates to remember are the date by
which payment must be received – you should allow four
working days for the money to reach them – and the date your
statement is sent out. Try to time your credit card purchases
just before or on the usual statement date in order to get up to
56 days' interest-free credit.

17 If you are the forgetful type, you would be better off settling credit card accounts by direct debit from an interest-paying current account.

18 If you are a forgetful *and* impecunious person, give up credit cards altogether and see the difference it can make to your financial situation.

19 Never sign a credit card slip without checking that the amount you are authorising appears in the 'total' column. Blank total boxes give less than honest traders the opportunity to enter a higher amount later. Restaurants seem to be particularly guilty of this, adding an unauthorised service and cover charge. Always keep your copy of the sales voucher which will be your proof that the total was added or changed after you had signed the top copy of the voucher.

20 When buying goods costing over £100 you get double indemnity if you pay by credit card. It therefore makes sense to use your credit card when ordering goods through the post or when having to pay in advance. If the goods then fail to arrive, or the supplier goes out of business before you receive them, the credit card company will reimburse you. This protection only applies to credit cards and not charge cards or gold cards.

Income Tax

21 If income tax demands become overdue they can accrue interest. If you can't pay a demand by the due date, it's worth finding out whether the interest rate charged by the Inland Revenue is less than the cost of an overdraft from your bank.

22   To enable you to fill in your tax form and take advantage of tax free allowances and investments without employing the services of an accountant, get a copy of *The Allied Dunbar Tax Guide* by W I Sinclair, published annually by Longman. The Consumers' Association also produce an annual guide called *Which? Way to Save Tax*, and Piatkus publish a useful book on *Perfectly Legal Tax Loopholes*. They should all be available at your local library.

23   Students who take part-time jobs to eke out their grant are likely to have tax deducted, leaving them with the hassle of recovering it. To avoid this, fill in the Inland Revenue Form P38S. Find out the current tax free limit and allowances, and how you will be taxed if you exceed the limit, by studying the Inland Revenue Leaflet IR60 *Income Tax and Students* from your nearest Inland Revenue offices.

Insurance

○ *Advice*

24   It pays to shop around for insurance to get the best cover at the best price. List the things you really need to cover – household buildings and contents, car insurance, etc – and present these items to various companies for quotes. If you need advice, ask your bank to put you in touch with their insurance adviser, or find an insurance broker through the Yellow Pages, or through The British Insurance Brokers Association (telephone 071-623 9043) who will supply a list of members in your area.

25   Registered brokers are bound by a code of conduct to put your interests first, as opposed to insurance salesmen who are paid to convince you that theirs is the only company worth considering. Brokers will still get commission from the company they introduce you to, so you shouldn't have to pay them a fee, but make sure about this from the outset.

26   Building societies will insist you take out buildings insurance
at the time your home is mortgaged. If you don't have a
mortgage it still makes sense to protect your biggest asset with
the maximum cover at the best possible rates. Send for the
leaflet *Buildings Insurance for Home Owners* from The Association of British Insurers, Aldernay House, Queen Street,
London EC4N 1TT.

○   *Home contents insurance*

27   Indemnity insurance is the cheapest type and means that the
insurance company will pay for the repair of damaged articles
or the replacement of those stolen or destroyed, but only to
their value at the time of the incident. Policies which replace
new for old are more expensive but can often be the better bet.

28   If you haven't made any claims over the last year, try to
negotiate for a no-claims discount when you renew the policy.

29   Some insurance companies give special discounts for home
contents insurance if you have installed a burglar alarm or
have taken other measures to protect your home – by fitting
smoke detectors for example.

○   *Health insurance*

30   Private health insurance may seem like the ultimate luxury to
those who are hard pressed financially. BUPA have intro-
duced a budget plan offering cut-price access to private health
if an operation cannot be done on the NHS in six weeks. You
still get a nightly allowance, or half of that for day care surgery,
whether you are treated on the NHS or not. For information
contact BUPA, Provident House, Essex Street, London
WC2R 3AX. Telephone 071-353 5212.

31　The larger private medical insurers tend to blame the increased cost of medical care for the recent hefty rise in annual premiums (often by more than a third). As well as the better known BUPA and PPP there are over 30 other medical insurance companies who offer similar services at very competitive rates, so it is well worth shopping around. You could cut corners by inviting a broker to list the options for you.

○ *Life insurance*

32　It's vital not to allow payments for a life insurance policy to lapse, so take care to make any necessary arrangements if you change address or move your bank account.

33　You can lose a great deal of money if you cash in a life insurance policy before it reaches maturity, so consider the options and financial commitments very carefully before you sign on the dotted line.

○ *Motor insurance*

34 As with all other types of insurance it pays to shop around for the best deal. Many companies offer discounts if you elect to pay a voluntary excess (say the first £50) of a claim, or if you take out an owner driver or named drivers policy *(see 36)*.

35 Some insurance companies offer special rates for women drivers or for cars fitted with an alarm or security marking (such as the vehicle registration number etched on the windows). You may be able to get a special deal if you have a second car in the family insured with the same company.

36 Where you have insurance for named drivers only, don't let others persuade you to let them drive your car on the basis that their own insurance covers them. It is most likely limited to third party only, even on a comprehensive policy, and if the borrower accidentally damaged your car you could be faced with the repair bill.

37 Premiums for young drivers are exceedingly high. Since young drivers tend to have relatively inexpensive cars it will probably be more economical in the long run to insure for third party, fire and theft only.

Legal Help

38 Those of less than moderate means can get legal aid for all sorts of problems including divorce, debt, social security claims and criminal charges. Your local Citizens Advice Bureau (CAB) will help you determine both financially and legally whether or not you are eligible. If you do qualify they will put you in touch with a solicitor in your area who deals with legal aid (not all do).

39 Many solicitors offer a fixed-fee interview, which provides half an hour of legal advice for a small set fee. Names of solicitors who provide this service are listed in the *Solicitors' Regional Directory* (available from libraries, Citizens Advice Bureaux and local advice centres). It pays to find someone who specialises in your particular type of legal dispute.

40 After an accident of any kind you can get free legal advice on whether you have a claim for compensation. Under the Accident Legal Advice Service (ALAS), a solicitor will give you a free interview and can advise you whether you have a good case. Names of solicitors who provide this service are listed in the *Solicitors' Regional Directory (see 39)*. Or contact The Law Society, Accident Legal Advice Service, Freepost, London WC2A 1B2. Telephone 071-242 2430.

41 Rights of Women, an organisation of female lawyers, offers free legal advice to women. They also produce leaflets on such matters as domestic violence. Advice is by phone or letter only – no callers. Rights of Women, 52 Featherstone Street, London EC1 8RT. Telephone 071-251 6577.

42 Small claims for damages (up to £1,000) are heard by district judges, and the process is quick and simple to enable people to present their case without a solicitor. The claim must be made to the court in the area where the event occurred or where the defending party are situated. It often helps to have an initial consultation with a solicitor to assess your chances of winning *(see 39)*.

43 Contrary to popular belief you don't have to go to a solicitor to make a will. Oxfam's *Wills Pack* gives you all the advice you need. Write to them at 274 Banbury Road, Oxfordshire OX2 7DZ. Alternatively the Consumers' Association produce an action pack called *Make Your Will (see 229 for address)*.

See also 474.

Telephone Tips

Reducing Costs

44 Resolve to keep telephone conversations to the absolute minimum and see the difference it makes to your next quarterly bill. Only ring friends who are given to lengthy chats just before you have to go out or when you are expecting someone to visit, then you will have a good reason to keep it short and sweet without causing offence.

45 If you lose track of time when talking on the phone, keep an egg timer nearby and use it to remind you when you've had 3 or 4 minutes.

46 Don't have an answering machine unless you need one to receive important business calls. Nine out of 10 callers will want you to ring them back whether or not you want to or can afford to.

47 It pays to be disciplined about using the phone in off-peak hours. The cheap rate runs from 6 pm until 8 am Monday to Friday, all day Saturday and Sunday plus Christmas Day, Boxing Day and New Years' Day. Don't make the mistake of thinking bank holidays are an extension of the cheap weekend – they are in fact treated as a normal weekday. The standard rate applies from 8 am until 9 am and from 1 pm until 6 pm Monday to Friday. At the peak time, 9 am until 1 pm Monday to Friday, even local calls can be as much as five times dearer.

48 A very quick call at the off-peak rate can work out cheaper than the cost of sending a letter. To make the most of your time, jot down notes beforehand to remind you to cover everything you need to say, and don't waste time summarising or repeating yourself unless absolutely necessary.

49 Beware of messages to call people on 0860 or 0836 numbers – these are the cellular network codes for car and mobile phones and you will be charged a much higher rate. Wait until they call you back, or at least until they can be reached on an ordinary phone.

50 Be firm when you are asked to hang on because the person you want is on another line or they have to look up information in files or whatever. Ask if Mr X could call you back when he is free, or Mrs Y to return the call when she has the details of your query to hand. If they can't do this it is usually still cheaper to make another call later than to hold on.

| 51 | It is cheaper to make a very quick call to another party to ask them to call you back than to make a reverse charge call. |

| 52 | If you rarely make outgoing calls on your phone, you may qualify for a low-user rental rebate. You will be eligible for a 25% discount if you use less than 120 units each quarter. As an alternative to the low-user rebate, BT has introduced the Support Line scheme for those whose quarterly bills stay below a certain amount exclusive of rental. The rental charge is reduced by half and 30 free calls are credited to the account each quarter. If, however, Support Line users go above the 120 unit maximum, the extra units are charged at a higher than normal rate. To find out more about low cost rebates and Support Line services, ring Freephone 0800 800 862. |

○ **Extension kits**

| 53 | You don't have to be a DIY buff to install your own phone extension and save on expensive callout and installation charges. Look in Yellow Pages under 'Telephone Shops' for stockists of extension kits and the whole range of BT approved telephones, including cordless phones, payphones, carphones and numerous accessories. |

Bills

| 54 | If your policy is not to pay your phone bill until the red bill arrives, don't cut it too fine. Most subscribers are allowed between 35-40 days after the first bill is sent out before they are cut off, but personal records of payment are taken into account. The reconnection fee will be many times the interest you might have earned by delaying payment. If you are expecting a bill to arrive when you will be on holiday or even in hospital, BT will most likely be sympathetic if given prior warning. |

55   If you feel you have been overcharged, put your complaint in writing and send it in with an amount you think is reasonable. If you withhold payment completely you risk being cut off, which means you'd have to pay to be reconnected. BT will check meter readings, compare previous quarters' charges and look through their records of faults affecting your line. Your bill will be re-adjusted if they think the complaint is justified.

Special Services

56   There is a call barring facility which is especially handy if there's a chance that teenagers, lodgers, builders or babysitters will use the phone in your absence. You must be connected to a modern digital exchange (ask the operator) and for a reasonable quarterly charge you can elect to bar all outgoing calls from your number other than emergency 999 calls and 151 (faults) calls. Or you can bar all but local calls. You can also ask for call barring just on premium rate services such as the 0898 lines – and this will be done for you free of charge.

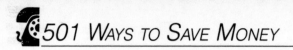

Note *Many people are already connected to a modern digital exchange and by 1995 it is expected that the whole of the country will be on one. The operator will be able to tell you if your exchange is a digital one.*

| 57 | It can save money to make a person-to-person call if you are uncertain whether the person you wish to talk to will be found at that number. Although it costs more than normal if the person in question can speak to you, it costs nothing if they are unavailable and someone else answers. Consider this option if making expensive long-distance or overseas calls, and if there is a good chance that the person you require will be unavailable.

| 58 | ADC (Advice of Duration and Charge) calls can add quite a bit to your bill as they require the services of an operator, but if you are on a modern digital exchange and have a Touch Tone telephone *(see 62)* you can do it yourself for a fraction of the cost. To get charge advice, press the 'star' button followed by 40, then the 'star' button again. Now dial the number you want. When you have finished talking and replaced the receiver, the phone will ring and a recorded announcement will tell you the cost of the call. For further information about the do-it-yourself ADC service call Freephone 0800 800 150.

○ *Directory Enquiries*

| 59 | Nowadays you are automatically charged if you call Directory Enquiries on your private line, and you are entitled to two numbers for the standard charge. If you call Directory Enquiries from a call box, however, it's *free* to everyone.

| 60 | The Directory Enquiry service is still free at all times to the blind and disabled, who need to apply for a PIN (Personal Identification Number). Ring 0800 919195 for details.

61 | An independent Talking Pages service now operates in some parts of the country and can be cheaper to use than Directory Enquiries, especially if you need information about particular services. You only pay for the duration of the call and that can be kept to the minimum if you are brief and to the point when explaining what you want. For more information on how to use Talking Pages, telephone (0734) 506707.

o **_Alarm calls_**

62 | Alarm calls are expensive and soon mount up. It would be cheaper to buy an alarm clock than book regular alarm calls. However, if you are on a modern digital exchange *(see note after 56)* and have a Touch Tone telephone you can give yourself an alarm call. Press the 'star' button then 55 then 'star' again, then the required time of the call (eg for half past seven in the morning, press 0730), then the 'hash' or 'gate' symbol. You will automatically be called at the pre-set time. If you want to cancel, press 'star' 55 then 'hash' or 'gate'. For further information on alarm call services call Freephone 0800 800 150.

Faults

63 | When you buy a telephone it should be covered by a one year guarantee. If it stops working after that, try this simple check to find out where the fault lies and save on call out charges. Unplug it and try another phone in the same socket. (Borrow one from a neighbour if necessary.) If the second phone works, then your suspicions about the original one are confirmed. If the second phone doesn't work the line is most probably at fault. Check whether you have overloaded the system by installing too many extra phones and sockets for the line to cope with. Unplug all but one phone and see if this works on its own. If it does, keep adding phones, up to a maximum of four, to see how many the system can cope with. Ask a friend, a kindly operator, or the BT engineers on 151 to assist you by ringing your number.

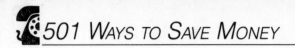

64　Once established that a fault has occurred on the line, BT has an obligation to repair it by the next working day after it is reported. Unless they can prove circumstances beyond their control prevented a call out – you and your telephone line were trapped under 6 feet of snow in the Cairngorms, for example – you can claim compensation of one month's line rental charge for each working day they fall short of installation and repair targets. You can also claim the same level of compensation if a BT engineer fails to turn up for an agreed appointment to install an exchange line.

65　Never make calls via the operator if you can possibly avoid it as they cost considerably more than dialling direct. If, however, you are asking for the operator's assistance because you keep getting crossed or noisy lines, cut off, or not the number you dialled, then inform the operator what has happened and ask them to make allowances on your phone bill for the wasted calls. You do need to ask them to do this – it doesn't happen automatically when calls go wrong.

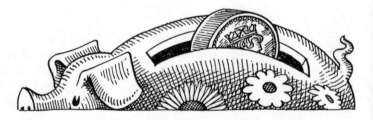

DIY and Home Maintenance

Equipment

66 Many tools have to be written off when rust sets in. If storing tools indefinitely, protect them by rubbing the metal parts with a coating of petroleum jelly then rolling up in brown paper. Label the package for future reference.

67 When buying a ladder, the wooden 'combination' type is probably the best investment as it can be used as simple steps or a triple extension, or converted into scaffolding and used as a pair of trestles to support a plank.

○ *Hiring equipment*

 It makes sense to hire rather than buy tools which you'll only use occasionally, such as floor sanders, wallpaper steamers, carpet stretchers, garden strimmers and the like. Look up members of the Hire Association of Europe (HAE) under 'Hire Services' in Yellow Pages.

 To get value for money when hiring equipment, have all the preparations for the job done before you collect the equipment.

 Ask about weekend rates when hiring tools – they often work out at only fractionally more than a daily rate, enabling you to get maximum use of the tools or to share costs with a friend or neighbour who is planning similar projects.

Materials

 Don't buy plaster if you only need it to fill tiny holes and cracks – use toothpaste instead. When set hard it can be sanded down, if a wet finger hasn't done a good job of smoothing it previously.

 Get the last squeeze from a tube of bath sealant by immersing it in hot water for a few minutes before using.

Save leftovers of putty by wrapping in kitchen foil and storing in the fridge. It will remain usable for up to a year.

Don't throw away aerosol cans if they clog up before the contents are finished. Remove the nozzle and place in boiling water for a couple of minutes if the contents are soluble. If the aerosol contains oil-based paint leave the nozzle overnight in paraffin or paintstripper.

75 Expensive anti-condensation crystals are money down the drain. Salt or charcoal are much cheaper and do a good job of absorbing moisture. To dry out a damp room, divide 2 lb (900g) of coarse kitchen salt among four tins and place each one in a corner of the room. When the salt is saturated with moisture, dry it out by sitting the tins on a warm stove. The salt is ready for use again when dry.

76 Protect rubber gloves when doing heavy-duty DIY work by turning them outside in and putting strips of sticking plaster inside each fingertip. This will also protect them from long fingernails.

Painting

77 Cheap brands of paint are actually a false economy as you will usually need more of the paint to get good coverage. Buy the best you can afford and follow the manufacturer's instructions for preparing the surface beforehand.

78 One of the greatest inventions in recent years is the miniature tester pots of paint. With some brands you will even get the cost back if you buy the full-size tin. When testing the colour, paint it round corners to see how it looks in both light and shade. Test pots are the perfect size when you want just a small amount of paint, for example to paint a picture frame.

79 Paintbrushes can be cleaned with paraffin instead of the more expensive cleaners sold specifically for the purpose. Suspend the brushes in a jar so that any paint residue sinks to the bottom and the clear liquid can be poured off and used again.

80 Together with Jimmy Watts, a specialist in painting techniques, I recently made two home videos on decorative paint finishes. Launched at the Ideal Home and Daily Telegraph Period Homes exhibitions, the videos were snapped up by elegant, well-off ladies who'd just received estimates for specialist painting that were on a par with the National Debt. The biggest customers were self-employed painters and decorators who proudly told us that they could charge thousands of pounds for these skills which *they* had yet to learn! Video 1 covers rag rolling, dragging and stippling, while Video 2 shows marbling, two-tone rag rolling, splattering, tortoiseshelling and woodgraining. If you would like copies, contact Box Top Video Productions, 69 Fairfax Road, London NW6 4EE. Telephone 071-625 4476/7/8. Mention to them that you have a copy of this book and they will give you a special discount.

81 To increase coverage and make paint go on better, stand the tin upside down for a few hours at room temperature before using. Make sure the lid is on securely first. Enamel paint will thin down and so go further and give a better porcelain-like finish if the tin is left in a bowl of hot water for half an hour.

Tiling

82 Cork tiles are cheaper than vinyl, but just as durable. They are easy to lay and give a warmer surface. Seal untreated cork tiles with a clear varnish for easy cleaning and an attractive finish. Sheet cork does a good inexpensive cover-up job on old ceramic tiled surfaces such as basin surrounds, bathroom window sills, etc.

83 If you can't afford to retile, use ceramic tile paint to give an inexpensive new look.

84 Where grout is discoloured, there's no need to go to the expense and bother of regrouting. Instead paint over the grout with special grout paint, after scrubbing off stains with a toothbrush dipped in household bleach.

85 If the tiles themselves need revamping, try the following inexpensive tile cleaner which will remove soap deposits and hard water scale and leave tiles looking like new. Put 1 cup of bicarbonate of soda in a plastic bowl together with 1 cup ammonia, 1/2 cup vinegar and 14 cups of warm water. Cover tightly and shake thoroughly to mix. Apply neat using a plastic mesh scourer *(see 186)* to dislodge stubborn marks. Rinse well with a sponge and plenty of clear warm water laced with a little vinegar. Polish with a soft dry cloth.

86 Plain white ceramic tiles are usually cheaper than coloured or patterned ones. If you think the effect would be too clinical, frame each tile using brightly coloured grout, or stencil a design on them using ceramic tile paint. The joy of plain white, on the other hand, is that it shows off everything else so well and with just a few plants and brightly coloured towels or accessories can look stunning.

Dry Rot, Fungus and Pests

87 The longer you leave wood infestation, dry rot or other damp induced deterioration, the more rapidly it will take hold and the bill to cure it will be larger. Only deal with reputable, well-established firms who are less likely to go bankrupt than the one-man band. All work should be guaranteed, but the guarantee will be worthless if the firm goes out of business.

88 Dry rot can be treated by painting it with petrol until it blackens and dies. Work in a well-ventilated atmosphere, and don't smoke.

89 Specialist companies dealing with rot and insect attack should offer you a free survey. They will then quote either for doing the job for you, or for supplying the appropriate products for you to do it yourself. Look under 'Pest and Vermin Control' in the Yellow Pages.

Security

90 If you don't have the means to install a home alarm, put up a dummy box instead. Paint the outside of a biscuit tin bright yellow, write 'Modern Alarm' in black on the bottom and fix to an outside wall. Joining a Neighbourhood Watch scheme and displaying their stickers in a prominent window is also an effective deterrent to burglars.

91 Yale-type locks are easily opened by would-be intruders using nothing more than a credit card. Prevent this by pushing a few drawing pins into the inside edge of the wooden door frame just in front of the lock.

Baths

92 Special bath cleaners are a waste of money. For everyday cleaning use a squirt of washing-up liquid on an old long-handled back brush. To remove ingrained tidemarks on plastic baths, use silver polish. Stains on enamel baths can be shifted with salt, white spirit, vinegar or paraffin.

93 Paraffin or bicarbonate of soda will break down corrosion around taps and other chrome bathroom fittings.

94 If an enamel bath is in a really awful state of repair and you can't afford to replace it, look up 'Bath restorers' in Yellow Pages and ask for a quote. They can give enamel baths an amazing new lease of life for less than the cost of a new one.

Cookers and Hobs

95 Bicarbonate of soda can be used as a 'sealer' on a newly cleaned over. Spread a light film over the surfaces using a damp cloth to make cleaning a doddle next time.

96 If faced with a really filthy oven you may have to resort to using caustic soda, which is the cheapest grime shifter for ovens and drains. First try heating the oven then switching it off, and while it's still warm place a small container of ammonia on the top shelf and a large container of boiling water on the bottom shelf. Close the door and leave overnight. Next day open the doors and windows to disperse the ammonia fumes and wash out the oven with soapy water. Apply bicarbonate of soda on a damp cloth for persistent stains – it's particularly good on glass doors.

97 Stains on a ceramic cooker top will respond to a soaking in hot vinegar. Leave it for at least ten minutes before wiping off. Repeat as necessary. Remember that vinegar when heated will rapidly boil up and expand, so always use with caution.

98 Cooker tops will be easier to clean if salt is sprinkled on spills as soon as they occur.

99 Where heavily encrusted stains on ceramic hobs and cookers have been well and truly welded on, cover with a layer of dishwashing or ordinary washing powder, place a wet kitchen towel over it and leave overnight. The next day work on it with a redundant credit card to scrape off the gunge.

Simple Furnishing Ideas

○ *Beds*

100 Apportion your spending money so that you can invest as much as possible on a good bed. Don't pay extra for so called 'Orthopaedic' beds, as there is no such thing. All well-made firm mattresses will give support to the back.

101 If you can't afford a new bed don't be tempted to replace just the mattress and keep the spring base, as the two will have deteriorated together. Instead consider buying a futon – a natural fibre mattress which is amazingly comfortable placed on any firm base such as the floor. When you roll it up each day you prolong its life by allowing air to circulate and any moisture to evaporate.

○ *Carpets and rugs*

102 Several thin coats of yacht varnish, allowed to dry thoroughly between coats, will build up to a tough protective and inexpensive cover for stairs. Alternatively, a runner is cheaper than fitted carpet. Remember to allow a good 18 inches (45.5cm) extra at the top and bottom and fold this under. When the treads wear, you can move the runner up to give new unworn risers. When the whole thing is threadbare, disguise a cord runner by laying a strip of brightly coloured canvas down the middle.

103 Big holes or indelible stains call for crafty surgery. Take a Stanley knife and neatly cut a square around the damaged part of the carpet. This will provide a template to cut out a matching square from a remnant. Also cut out a square of canvas 1 inch (2.5cm) larger than the template all round. Turn the damaged area of carpet back on itself and fix the square of canvas to the underside using a latex adhesive (such as Copydex). When the glue is completely dry, lay the carpet back in position and glue the underside of the new patch into the space.

104 It's a false economy to do without a felt underlay. It not only gives extra warmth but saves wear and tear on the carpet. Even a layer of newspaper under the carpet will be better than nothing to keep out draughts and give underfloor warmth.

105 Cheap, loosely woven carpets won't last any time at all in hard working areas. Buy the best you can afford for hallways and sitting room and spend less on dining room and bedrooms.

106 Visit one of the many Oriental rug warehouses to pick up the best bargains in floor coverings and wall hangings. Rugs are very useful if you're trying to sell your home – they look really luxurious and cosy on walls and do a terrific job of covering up holes and cracks, and you can always take them with you when you move.

107 Carpet samples can be bought very cheaply and make useful doormats for use inside the house to save wear and tear on vulnerable areas of fitted carpets. A few sewn together will form the basis of an attractive patchwork rug which can be made as big as you like in colours to tone in with your decor. They also make useful table protectors for sewing machines, typewriters and computers.

○ *Bedding*

108 When a sheet or blanket becomes worn in the centre, cut it in half (through the thin part down the middle) and reverse the halves, putting the middle to the outside and the outside to the middle. The centre seam can be quickly run up and the sides hemstitched.

109 You can very often pick up perfectly good eiderdowns in charity shops like Oxfam. If they don't match your decor, put them inside a duvet cover. Fix velcro strips or studs at the corners of the eiderdown and at the corresponding corners inside a suitably sized duvet cover.

110 You can make duvet covers out of sheet oddments bought at sales for less than the price of buying ready-made.

○ *Curtains*

111 It's sometimes cheaper and easier to make curtains from bargain priced sheets bought at sales. You not only get extra width, but ready stitched hems too.

112 When re-hanging washed or dry-cleaned curtains, change them round so that the previous outer edges now hang on the inside where they catch the light. This way they'll fade evenly and last much longer.

113 A long length of open-weave white muslin or similar material makes an ideal curtain for a bedroom or small sitting room when draped round a wooden pole and used in conjunction with a plain blind. The effect is quite luxurious for a fraction of the price of made curtains. The only sewing you have to do is a simple hem at each end.

○ *Table cloths*

114 Take the measurements of your table and buy a large enough oddment of multicoloured PVC. Fashionable and thrifty, it saves on washing powders as it wipes clean, and protects the table surface from spills. Squares of sticking plaster placed on the underside of the cloth where it meets the table's corners will reduce wear and extend its life. PVC table cloths are ideal for using on the ground as picnic cloths or to cover garden tables.

115 It can work out cheaper to buy a single or double sheet instead of a large tablecloth. You'll probably find more choice in colours and patterns, too.

○ *General*

116 Although comparatively inexpensive to buy, cork mats stain easily unless a coat of protective varnish is applied when they are new. You can give a new lease of life to old ones, or renovate a set bought at a jumble sale, by rubbing them over with coarse sandpaper wrapped around a block of wood.

117 Make table napkins, cot sheets, hand towels and face flannels from old sheets, tablecloths and bath towels. Even babies' terry towelling nappies, if in good condition, can be dyed and used as hand towels.

118 Pick up old deck chairs for a song, or recover your own old ones. Unpick the worn material and use as a pattern to buy the same amount of new material in a brightly striped canvas. Before recovering, repair any cracks or tighten loose joints in the frame and apply a coat of yacht varnish. Bind a strip of foam rubber round the bars at the top and bottom of the chair to take some of the strain off the cover.

119 DIY picture framing saves pounds and the range of kits starts with simple glass and clip packages. The alternative is to rummage in junk shops and jumble sales for cheap frames. *(See 78)*.

See also 240, 242, 244, 245, 247, 252 and 254.

Dealing with Tradesmen

Recently a single gentleman moved into a house – in Dorset as it happens, but it could have been anywhere. The plumbing was suspect, the wiring was dangerously outdated and the plaster was crumbling where condensation and damp were playing ducks and drakes with the walls. He set to with the aid of Yellow Pages to employ a small army of local tradesmen to put the place right. Nearly all of them overcharged for work which was below an acceptable standard. It will gladden the heart of the long suffering householder to know that the man was a 'plant' from the Trading Standards Authority and the errant tradesmen were charged with defrauding the public.

120 It really does pay to have a knowledge of DIY skills, whether you intend to do the job yourself or get someone else to do it for you. For instance if you are able to tell a repairman that the belt of your washing machine has broken and you'd like a replacement fitted, rather than simply saying that the machine has gone wrong, you will avoid handing a less than honest workman the chance to make a bit extra out of your ignorance.

See 121.

|121| Evening classes run by your local authority are enormously good value. You can learn basic skills in various trades and it is quite likely that any person you employ will have picked up the knowledge at such classes.

|122| Find a good honest tradesman, preferably by word of mouth, and stick to him. We've all heard horror stories where 'cowboys' replace one worn out part with another that isn't much better and will soon necessitate another call out. The customer, of course, is charged for a new part. It's most likely that a major component, a pump on a boiler for example, will carry a one year guarantee, so ask for the guarantee and keep it safely.

|123| When you ask a tradesman to call, first find out the minimum call out charge. This very often includes the first half hour of labour free, but do ask. Get an itemised bill for labour and replacement parts. If you feel you have been overcharged, report the matter to your local trading standards office.

|124| Always get written quotes from three to six different companies, before going ahead with any job which involves a substantial financial outlay. An estimate is a 'guesstimate and allows the Smart Alecs to stick a bit more on for 'unforeseen expenditure', so do specify a 'quote'. There is a rare chance that the cheapest will be the best, but there is a better chance that they are undercutting everyone else because they're desperate for work and could go out of business before the job is completed. A 20% difference in prices is the maximum you should consider.

|125| Although it is normal to be asked to pay something in advance for materials, you should never pay up-front for labour. Have the work priced item by item and pay as you go along, then if for any reason you wish to discontinue their services, you both know exactly where you are.

126 How many times have you made tea or coffee for a visiting tradesman, only to discover that he has added the time taken to drink it and engage in pleasant chit chat with you to your labour charges? Don't do it unless it's a day-long job. Does somebody rush to get you coffee when you've done an hour in the supermarket or have hardly taken your coat off at work?

127 Get tough. Women in dispute with men who are working for them often feel intimidated or are treated with barely disguised contempt. Tradesmen who undertake to do work for you have an obligation to turn up on time, do a decent job and to finish within agreed time limits. By failing to turn up or by arriving late they have broken part of the agreement. When paying the bill, deduct what you consider to be a reasonable amount for such things as phone calls to track them down, the cost of the launderette if they delayed coming to mend the washing machine, or perhaps the time you lost at your own work. Sometimes we get the service we deserve by paying out too freely for shoddy goods and services.

128 While a builders' work is in progress, you can check with a
spirit level to make sure that tiles or brickwork are running in
straight lines, that doors open and close properly and leave
enough clearance for carpets. Check that timber has been
jointed and glued, not just nailed together, that mitres are nice
and tight, and that you can hold a straight edge against any
plasterwork. Bad workmanship can then be corrected at the
worker's expense and will avoid more complex disputes later.
It does nothing for diplomatic relations if you stand, DIY
manual in hand, smugly pointing out flaws. Do the checks
when they've left for the day, and always state your grievances
in a reasonable and pleasantly firm manner.

129 Never be afraid to ask 'How much for cash?' when you're
quoted a price for a job, or where it might lead to a discount on
goods purchased. You'd be surprised how popular you become and how much better off financially as well.

Before Calling a Tradesman

130 Skill swapping saves money by trading your expertise and
labour with those of a neighbour or a friend. Perhaps they are
a dab hand at wallpapering and will agree to redecorate your
sitting room if you will make new curtains for them.

○ *Electrical appliances*

131 When an electrical appliance goes wrong, check for obvious
problems before calling help. The obvious things to check first
are the plugs, fuses and sockets. Always unplug the appliance
before investigating the causes.

○ *Washing machines, dishwashers and tumble driers*

132 A common fault on washing machines and dishwashers is a kink in the outlet hose – check that it is neither bent nor blocked. Also check the programme dials again and the obvious but often overlooked reason for a non-starter, that the water supply has been turned off. With washing machines and tumble driers, see if the filters are choked with fluff.

○ *Vacuum cleaners*

133 Check whether the bag is too full or has burst. Is the fan belt caught on something? If so, loosen and untangle it, or, if worn, buy a replacement. Is the suction tube blocked or damaged? Push an old uncurled metal coat hanger inside the tube to see if anything is stuck in it.

134 Even a partially blocked vacuum cleaner uses far more energy than one which is regularly cleaned out and free from fluff, so follow the manufacturer's instructions for changing filters and preventing blockages.

○ *Central heating system*

135 I was once told by a heating and plumbing expert that if he had a fiver for every time he was called out when the water was simply not switched on, a pilot light had gone out, or time controls hadn't switched themselves on following a power cut, he could retire early as a wealthy man. Call out charges are considerably more than a fiver these days, so it pays to double check with instructions before summoning costly help. A checklist for a central heating breakdown would read:

- Is the Pilot light still on? If not, relight following the manufacturer's instructions.
- Check the fuse on the main switch – likely to be adjacent to the programmer – and check that the time switch is in the 1-2, 3-4 sequence.
- Check the boiler and room thermostats – it may not be cold enough for the system to have switched on.
- Are there air locks in the pump or pipes . . .?

Saving Energy and Recycling

Insulation

136 Providing that it's installed by a reputable firm, double glazing can reduce heat loss by up to 50%, but the cost can be prohibitive. DIY double glazing is possible using plastic channels into which a pane of glass slides and is secured to the windows with special clips. Cheapest of all is sheet polythene which is the most elementary form of double glazing, but also acts as a safety measure if the glass gets broken. It comes in packs of different sizes, is easily trimmed with scissors and is made to adhere to the windows with the gentle heat of a hairdrier. Clingfilm is a reasonably good alternative.

137 Best bargains in insulating materials tend to be found in the summer months and once winter comes soon pay for themselves.

138   Because hot air rises, you can save up to 15% of heat loss by fitting a 2 inch (5 cm) thick fibreglass insulating blanket (a double layer if you can afford it) in the loft. Alternatively pack with a 4 inch (10 cm) layer of loose-fill granules. In terms of saving fuel, the material will pay for itself in two years.

139   If your home was built before 1976 and has no loft insulation or insulation that's less than 12 inches (30 mm) thick, you could be eligible for a council grant of up to 90% of the approved cost of loft insulation. You must apply before the work is carried out.

140   Insulate under a sloping roof, round the loft hatch and on top of the trap door but never under the cold water tank as the warmth from below will help prevent a freeze. The tank itself needs a jacket, also to prevent freezing.

141   A very cost effective exercise is to insulate pipes which lead from the hot water cylinder to the taps, and those running under floorboards.

142   Buying a jacket – or even two – for your hot water tank will greatly reduce fuel bills. If the budget won't stretch to the real McCoy then a double layer of corrugated cardboard taped or tied round the cylinder will do the job pretty well.

143   Where draughts are whistling through badly fitting windows, close the gap with a silicone-based sealant. These come in a plastic bottle with nozzle for easy application. Open the window and apply an even layer around the inner frame. Immediately close the window to press the sealant well in, then open it again until the sealant dries.

144   Don't lose expensive heat up the chimney. When not in use cover fireplaces with a plywood or plasterboard panel cut to size and painted. If you're blocking off a fireplace permanently, have the chimney capped or build in a ventilator to prevent damp.

145   Cavity wall insulation can save up to half the heat lost through badly insulated walls. This is not a job for the DIY enthusiast to tackle as some materials are toxic and can cause skin allergies. Find an approved contractor in your area by contacting The National Cavity Insulation Association, PO Box 12, Haslemere, Surrey GU27 3AN. Telephone (0428) 54011.

146   In winter replace ordinary light bulbs in cold areas such as lavatories, utility rooms and porches with 'heat and light' bulbs. They cost very little to run and provide just enough warmth to prevent freezing conditions.

Central Heating

147 To maintain the efficiency of your central heating system have it serviced at least once a year. You can assist matters greatly yourself by letting the pump run for a couple of minutes each month throughout the summer.

148 Heating accounts for more than one third of your total energy bill, so it pays to have an efficient system. The average efficient life span of a central heating boiler is ten years. An old and inefficient appliance can waste so much money that a replacement could see an immediate 10% saving in your fuel bills.

149 Before installing central heating it is vital to get quotes from several reliable companies as well as a firm 'completion' date. *(See 124.)* You often get better deals in summer when demand is lower. Radiators and thermostats are costly to resite, so plan exactly where you want them positioned before the job starts. Radiators are traditionally sited under windows, with the result that expensive heat is lost out of the window. And if the curtains are long enough to stop draughts, they also interfere with the heat flow when drawn, redirecting the heat up over the cold window pane. Thermostats in a draughty hallway cannot work efficiently. A rush of cold air when doors are opened will produce a noticeable drop in temperature. They also react to heat spots, so don't position them near a record player, lamp or TV.

150 By fitting individual thermostatic radiator valves to every radiator in your home you can dispense with all other thermostats, except the one on the boiler. Have them fitted when your central heating is installed or at the annual service when the radiators are drained. They save heat by allowing each room to be controlled separately. Turn the thermostats right down in rooms that aren't used, like spare bedrooms.

151   If you have a choice, never put a fridge or freezer near a heat-giving appliance such as a cooker, or radiator. When space is limited or you have no option, leave a gap between them or put insulating material fixed to a board between them.

152   Check that you are not overheating rooms. Each 1°C (about 2°F) change in the room thermostat setting will make a difference of between 6 and 10% to your heating costs. Most people could lower the temperature a few degrees without noticing, or could wear extra clothing instead of turning up the thermostat.

153   Electric storage heaters work at night building a reserve of heat at off peak electricity rates and releasing it into the room the following day and evening. The Economy 7 electricity system does not help unless you are really sure you can run appliances and heating at off peak times.

154   If you go away for long periods, consider fitting a frost thermostat to the outside of the house. It activates the heating system when the temperature drops to a very low level and pipes are in danger of freezing.

155   Once you are in bed, you don't need a high room temperature. If you turned in 30 minutes earlier throughout the winter, there would be a substantial improvement in heating costs and quite likely in your health too. If the heat is on all night it can add at least 15% to the heating bill. The exception might be in severe weather, unless you have a frost thermostat to activate the system *(see 154)*. Lowering the temperature a few degrees and keeping a constant low heat rather than bursts of higher temperature can work out almost as cheaply and give the house a gentle uniform warmth.

156   Radiator foil, although not cheap to buy, can save up to 15% on your heating bills. It prevents the heat from disappearing through thin outside walls and heating the air outside. A cheaper alternative is to tape kitchen foil behind radiators and to the underside of any shelves situated a few inches above them. This will reflect heat back into the room.

Hot Water

157   Around one-fifth of your total fuel bill goes on hot water. In summer if you have the choice between using an immersion heater or the central heating boiler to heat the water the latter will most likely be cheaper.

158   Wise use of an immersion heater can save money. Whether it is more economical to leave the immersion heater on all the time or switch it on only when you need hot water will depend on the individual household and the number of people at home all day. If it has a timer, it would work out cheaper to have it on once or twice a day only if there is no one at home during the day. Programme the water to switch on just before you get up and again before you come home. Where water is needed throughout the day at odd times, it may be cheaper to leave it on and allow it to regulate itself when it reaches the required temperature. It is worth trying each option for several weeks at a time, making a note of the electricity reading on your meter at the beginning and end of each trial period, and comparing the difference. Choose times when there will be normal usage of hot water – avoiding, for example, holiday times, when guests come to stay, and very cold spells.

159   If you use your immersion heater on an 'only as needed' basis, turn it off before you get into the bath (unless someone else wants a bath after you).

160   A shower saves hot water and so reduces your fuel bills – four or five people can shower in the same amount of hot water needed for a single bath.

161   Turn down the thermostat on the hot water cylinder to 60°C (140°F) or less. It is pointless and a waste of money to keep bathwater so hot it can scald you, and you have to add so much cold water that the bathroom becomes a sauna.

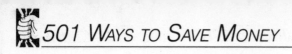

Fuel

 Central heating oil tends to fluctuate in price according to such things as a crisis in the world oil market or a seasonal decrease in demand. Always ring around at least three local suppliers before placing your order. You generally get a better rate the bigger your order is, and it's worth asking for a discount for paying the delivery man rather than waiting for an invoice. Coal and logs are also cheaper in summer when demand is lower.

163 Always store coal in a dark shed or bunker. Exposed to the daylight it will rapidly deteriorate and crumble to dust.

164 Coal will go further if a good handful of washing soda is dissolved in a bucket of warm water and then thrown over each hundredweight as it is delivered.

Lighting

165   Don't keep switching fluorescent lights on and off when you leave the room if it's only for a short time. These lights use more energy to relight than to stay lit for short periods. Although fluorescent tubes may be more expensive to buy than ordinary 100 watt bulbs, they last ten times longer and cost only half as much to run.

166   Dimmer switches can prolong the life of standard bulbs and can cut the running costs by as much as 75%. It's unlikely that you would have to spend money on alterations to your existing wiring.

Domestic Appliances

○ *Washing machines, dishwashers and tumble driers*

167   Only use a washing machine or dishwasher when you have a full load, or if you have one, make use of the economy, half-load wash when you need things in an emergency. The cooler the wash temperature, the cheaper the cost, and with a washing machine it's kinder to your clothes too. Soaking the dirty items in plain cold water for a few hours before loading the machine is a cheap and efficient method of loosening dirt.

168   You don't need the pre-soak and hot wash cycle for dirty clothes if you programme your washing machine for a shorter cycle at a lower temperature. Turn it off at the point in the cycle where the water and soap are mixed through. Leave the load to soak for a few hours or overnight for the dirt to dissolve. Switch back on and allow the cycle to continue. The clothes will be just as clean for half the cost.

169   Washing machines which only take in cold water and heat it to the required temperature are less economical to run than those which make use of already heated water from your hot water system.

170   Save energy by turning a tumble drier off half-way through its recommended drying time and leaving the clothes in the warm drum to finish off on 'free'heat.

See also 131, 132 and 135.

o   **Kettles and irons**

171   Appliances which have a build-up of hard water scale cost more to run. If you live in a hard water area, de-scale kettles, steam irons and immersion heaters frequently.

172   De-scale a kettle by half filling it with equal parts of vinegar and water. It is essential that this mixture never comes beyond the half-way mark as the vinegar expands when heated and could cause burns by spurting out of the spout and top. Boil for a couple of minutes then leave the liquid to cool in the kettle. Rinse out thoroughly.

173   To de-scale an iron, carefully pour white vinegar into the steam channel when the iron is still warm but switched off. Leave until the sediment dissolves. Drain and refill with boiled or distilled water (from defrosting the fridge) or rainwater and use the steam button (still with the iron switched off) until all residue is rinsed out.

174   Once de-scaled, keep a well scrubbed sea shell in the bottom of a kettle to attract scale. A few glass marbles will also prevent the build-up of scale.

See also 239 and 251.

○ *Freezers and cookers*

 Try to remember to switch off electric cookers before the end of cooking time. This is not recommended for bread, cakes and other items where cooking times and temperatures must be exact, but works well for roasts and casseroles – switching off 15 minutes early and leaving the oven door closed will finish the dish off perfectly.

176 As soon as you spot worn seals on fridges, freezers and ovens replace them. Worn seals will mean an inefficient appliance and a waste of energy.

You'll cut the cost of running your freezer by 10% if you defrost it regularly (at least twice a year). To make defrosting easier next time, after defrosting and cleaning and before filling it up again, rub glycerine on the inside surfaces.

178 A freezer is most economical to run when full, but this needn't mean buying extra items which you don't actually need. Shop around for a bumper lot of cut-price loaves at the end of the day, or week, from bakers and supermarkets. Or fill milk cartons and margarine tubs with water and freeze into blocks of ice to use in cold boxes or to keep bottles cold in summer. Or make and store handy ice cubes *(see 370)*.

See also 151, 225, 226 and 228.

○ *Battery-operated appliances*

179 If you use a variety of battery-operated tools, and equipment, invest in nickel cadmium rechargeable batteries which can be recharged up to 1,000 times (equivalent to around 4 years) as opposed to the ordinary zinc chloride type which have a life span of 100 hours.

180 Listening to a battery-powered radio for just two hours a day costs you forty times more than if you plugged it into mains electricity.

Recycling

 Save on buying J Cloths by recycling them up to 5 times each. Add them to your towel wash in the washing machine, or to the cutlery basket in the dishwasher.

182 There's no need to spend money on plastic bottle stoppers if
you save the tops of sherry bottles. And if you boil a cork for a
minute until it becomes soft and pliable it will refit its bottle.

183 It's a waste of money to buy pedal bin liners when you get an
ample supply of free plastic carrier bags from supermarkets
and shops. Knot the handles together when they're full.

184 Use greaseproof paper instead of the more pricey tin foil
whenever you can. When you do use tin foil, recycle untorn
pieces by washing and drying carefully.

185 The inner greaseproof paper bags from cereal packets can be
cut up to make rings for the tops of jam jars or to place
between homemade hamburgers and pancakes before freezing. Alternatively use the bags whole to store bread, buns or
whatever else needs a good stout wrapper to keep it fresh.

186 Don't throw away the plastic mesh bags used to package
supermarket fruit. Roll up and use as scouring pads.

187 Save on buying envelopes and use those new ones sent with
junk mail. Stick a label over the printed address.

188 Instead of throwing away pencil stubs, cut them into suitable
lengths to make brilliant rawl plugs – the graphite in the lead
makes it easy for the hook or screw to enter the wood.

189 Keep empty rinsed out milk and other waxed cartons to use as
firelighters. Dried orange peel also makes a good firelighter.

Don't throw away plastic food containers such as cottage cheese and yoghurt tubs. With a few holes pierced in the bottom they make ideal pots for cuttings and seedlings. Use the bottom half of washing-up liquid bottles for sturdier pots to take bigger cuttings.

○ *Newspapers*

191 Old newspapers will make cheap bedding for pets, give extra insulation under floorboards and can be used to line troughs and holes when planting out in the garden.

192 Use dampened newspaper to clean windows with.

193 Make firelighters from rolled up sheets of newspaper, tied loosely in a knot. Place on the grate under dry wooden twigs. *(See also 189.)*

194 Save old newspapers, travel brochures, magazines, etc., to recycle as fuel bricks for the fire. Tear them up and soak them in
plenty of water until they become like pulp. Pull out handfuls
and squeeze out all the water to form balls. Leave in a warm
place to dry.

195 Newspapers can be turned into environmentally friendly plant
pots which can replace the more expensive peat variety. Like
peat, they will slowly disintegrate when placed in the ground,
feeding the soil. Use the bottom of a bottle as a mould and
paste broad strips of newspaper to it using a thin paste of flour
and water. Build up the layers until you have a thick pot shape.
Leave to dry then remove from the bottle.

○ **Egg boxes**

196 Use cardboard egg boxes as seed trays, planting one seed in
each individual compartment. When its time to plant out, just
put the box straight into the ground where it will eventually
disintegrate.

197 Cardboard egg boxes can be used on a fire to make coal burn
for longer. Place the coal inside the wet boxes and put on a fire
that is already well established.

See also 370.

Shopping on a Budget

Groceries

 Forward planning is the key to big savings. Wherever you can, try to set aside a bit from the housekeeping money so you don't miss out on bulk buys, special offers and seasonal bargains.

 Plan menus for the week alongside your food shopping list. This way you won't have to nip out for a forgotten essential ingredient and you only need buy what you'll use.

 Work out roughly how much money will cover the items you need before you go shopping, and leave credit cards and cheque book at home. That way you're forced to resist impulse buys.

201 | Although shopping early saves time and energy, the best bargains are found at the end of the day – particularly Saturdays – when prices are reduced for a quick sale.

202 | At all times, buying own-brand products will nearly always work out less than buying the equivalent well-known brands.

203 | Buying in bulk can result in sizeable savings but you need a lot of storage space and a freezer if the product is fresh. Things like sacks of carrots and baskets of mushrooms aren't a bargain if they're likely to go off before you can use them all. *(See 204 and 205.)*

204 | Sharing with friends is often the answer to bulk buying. In some cases, eg dog food and disposable nappies, if an order is big enough you can have it delivered direct from the manufacturers. If you and those around you know you will need a constant supply then it's worth a stamp or a quick phone call to find out if this is possible.

205 | When buying in bulk for the freezer choose vegetables in season as they will be cheap and plentiful. Picking your own fruit and vegetables works out cheaper than buying supermarket veg, which is often a good bit dearer than produce in farm shops.

206 | Although market stalls can provide bargains, make sure you aren't given old or bruised produce from behind the scenes. Check your goods before you leave the stall, and if they are of inferior quality ask for them to be changed.

207 | When buying citrus fruits which are priced per single piece, it isn't the size but the weight which gives you value for money. By balancing them in your hands you can tell which are the light, pithy ones and which are heavier and therefore contain more juice.

|208| Only go food shopping on a full stomach so you won't pile up the basket with extra mouthwatering snacks.

|209| It pays to be bold and ask for the scraps – not literally the stuff fit for the dustbin – but economy ends of bacon and cheese which are often seen sitting on trays behind the counter. You can get them for a fraction of the usual price, and you'd probably chop or grate them before cooking anyway.

|210| Bread which is a day or so old can be bought for half the price of fresh. It will taste freshly baked again if you sprinkle the top and bottom with water and put it into a hot oven for a couple of minutes.

|211| Cut-price stale buns and scones can be salvaged if you brush them over with milk and place them in a hot oven for two or three minutes. Served with butter and jam, they'll taste freshly baked.

|212| A lot of people hate scrounging for free or cut-price food, which is where the real or imagined family pet comes into its own – it's easier to ask for broken carrots and bags of greens if you say they're for the rabbits or hamsters, and the marrow bone and yesterday's bread rolls are for the dog. It's only when you ask for smoked salmon ends 'for the cat' that eyebrows may be raised!

|213| Where possible switch to cheaper substitutes – bacon pieces instead of whole rashers for a quiche, coley instead of cod for a fish pie. You'll get the same amount of flavour but for half the price. Family butchers and fishmongers score here for personal service and expert advice on the produce they sell.

214   Chicken portions are more expensive to buy per pound than whole chickens, and boneless, skinless fillets are the most expensive of all. Buy the complete bird and cut it up with kitchen shears or a sharp bladed knife. A friendly butcher might be persuaded to do it for you.

215   It's better to buy and immediately freeze fresh chickens which have been knocked down in price as they reach their sell-by date, than to buy ready-frozen birds which may contain 10% added water.

216   Take the butcher's advice on cheaper cuts of meat – belly or neck-end of pork and brisket; leg, flank, chuck and blade of beef; and breast or neck of lamb. With slow cooking and the addition of a dash of vinegar to help tenderise the meat, you can make delicious and nourishing casseroles and pot roasts.

217   Always check when you buy a larger size of something that it works out cheaper than buying duplicates of the smaller size. It usually does, but there are exceptions.

218   Where you can, buy items loose and save on the cost of packaging. This is one of the reasons for the success of The Body Shop and their refill system using the original containers. But chemists and family grocers will sell you many things, from rosewater to paraffin, for less if you take your own bottles and cans.

219   Economise by buying washing-up liquid in large economy sizes. But buy a good quality brand so you can water it down with an equal amount of water to make it go further. (Cheaper brands are less powerful and you'll use twice as much to do the work.) Decant into smaller containers for ease of use.

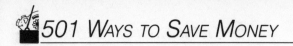
 If you buy washing soda in bulk instead of proprietary fabric softeners you'll also save money on washing powder. Add a teacupful of washing soda to clothes in the machine and you will need only half the recommended amount of washing powder.

 A tablespoon of vinegar in final rinsing water not only softens fabrics, but removes perspiration odours. Similarly, a dash of vinegar in the rinsing water will leave washing-up sparkling clean and bacteria free.

|222| Instead of buying special tubes of travel wash to take on holiday, simply decant some mild detergent, such as your usual washing-up liquid, into small plastic bottles, or use shampoo for washing your smalls when in transit.

|223| Save money by giving up liquid furniture polish and changing to solid wax polish which is two-thirds cheaper.

224 Herb teas are undoubtedly good for you but you pay a lot for the pretty packaging. Make any amount of herbal teas from fresh herbs grown in the garden, tubs or window boxes. Peppermint, rosemary, sage and camomile are among the most popular. They can be dried on a baking tray in the bottom of a warm oven or between layers of kitchen paper in a microwave.

See also 365 and 374.

Appliances

225 When deciding which type of appliance to buy it's worth considering the running costs as well as the purchase price. Gas cookers are more expensive to buy than electric ones, but cheaper to run. Cylinder vacuum cleaners are more economical to use than upright. A chest freezer costs very little less than an upright to run, but secondhand bargains can be found in reconditioned chest freezers because uprights are more popular.

226 Members of the Association of Manufacturers of Electrical Domestic Appliances (AMDEA) label their products to indicate how much each appliance will cost to run for a year. Imported (but often cheaper) models don't have this. As part of a scheme backed by the Energy Efficiency Office, fridges and freezers have a score from 1-10 to tell you which are the cheapest to run and least damaging to the environment. The higher the number, the more efficient the appliance.

227 Because TVs and videos are becoming more reliable it's no longer economical to hire them. For the cost of hiring them for just a few years you could have bought them new. But it still works out cheaper to hire items which you don't use every day, such as video cameras.

|228| Some retailers offer an extended warranty on their products beyond the normal one- or two-year guarantee period. This extended cover doesn't come cheap, so it's useful to know which appliances are more likely to break down than others. These days video recorders, washing machines and dishwashers are prone to break down far more than freezers, fridge freezers, tumble driers, microwave ovens, vacuum cleaners and TVs. According to the Consumers' Association, you are better off putting the money you would spend on these extended warranties in the bank and paying for the repairs if and when they occur. However, the choice is yours, and you may prefer to pay for peace of mind.

|229| When setting up home, list your most important purchases and read relevant back copies of the consumer magazine *Which?* These should be available in your local library. *Which?* is also available by subscription from The Consumers' Association, 2 Marylebone Road, London NW1 4DX. Telephone 071-486 5544.

|230| When replacing old appliances with new, it's worth asking for a trade-in deal on your old appliance, even if it's completely packed in.

Discount Scheme

|231| For a few pounds a year you can join 'Countdown', an organisation offering discounts at thousands of stores, hairdressers, restaurants, theatres, holiday and tour companies, financial services and car maintenance centres. Look to see if the red and blue Countdown signs are displayed by the local businesses you use before rushing to join, but the discounts are guaranteed and a couple can buy one membership card. The fee includes a quarterly magazine and discount guides. For further details contact Countdown, 88-92 Earl's Court Road, London W8 6EH. Telephone 071-938 1041.

Sales

232 It may pay you to travel to warehouse sales, Sunday markets and other such treasure troves. Get together with fellow bargain hunters to share petrol and split bulk buys. You can obtain information on sales and markets from The National Association of Wholesale Markets, 3 St Jude's Avenue, Mapperley, Nottingham.

233 Beware of one-day 'liquidation' sales and other apparently silly priced ruses. You can find genuine bargains on well-known makes here, but you can often be trapped by some of the biggest trading 'cons', such as when the original price on the ticket is put at a much higher figure than the normal retail price, making the cut-price offer seem irresistible. Frequently the best bargains go to the traders' friends, placed in the audience at mock auctions to encourage the unsuspecting to join in the bidding. By the time you discover you've been conned, the seller is far, far away. Think twice then think again before you buy, and if you do, make sure you get a proper receipt with the dealer's name and address on it – some are strangely reluctant to supply one.

234 The golden question to ask yourself when shopping in sales is 'Do I want it or need it?' Shoppers who are hard pressed for cash can only afford 'the needs' and must be ruthless about rejecting 'the wants', which probably wouldn't have half the appeal if you had to pay the full price for them.

Give goods labelled 'special purchase' a miss – on the whole they are not top quality goods but have been bought in cheaply by the stores to sell alongside the well known makes which do offer genuine discounts.

 Pay no attention to signs saying 'Sale goods cannot be exchanged or refunded'. The law says you have the same rights in the sales as at any other time. However if a fault has been pointed out to you before you bought the goods and clearly indicated as the reason for the price reduction, then a change of heart and subsequent complaint won't get you anywhere.

237 Big reductions can be found in glass and crockery at sales. 'Seconds' are often manufacturers' rejects but the flaw may be so slight that you would be unable to detect it in everyday use. Discontinued lines may be good value, but if anything gets broken you may not be able to replace it at a later date.

Secondhand Bargains

238 Don't get carried away by the description 'nearly new'. If an article is not new it is secondhand, whether the condition is excellent, good or fair. *Exchange and Mart* is not only good for buying or selling used or discount items but gives a good indication of prices too. Back issues of the Consumers' Association magazine *Which?* are essential reading to assess which goods stand the test of time. Your local library should have copies. *(See 229 for address.)*

239 Where you buy can be as important as what you buy and how much you pay. Secondhand kettles, water heaters and washing machines are not a good buy in hard water areas such as East Anglia, Essex, Gloucestershire, Hampshire, Kent, Lancashire, London, the West Midlands, Sussex, Wiltshire, parts of Yorkshire and north and south east Scotland.

240 In large cities phone your local branch of the Salvation Army to enquire about their sales of secondhand furniture.

241 When looking for secondhand items like a pair of skis, a particular camera, a shredder for the garden, etc., look in the relevant specialist magazines or contact local clubs and exhibitions. For instance, The Photographers' Gallery at 5 Great Newport Street, London WC2H 7HY (Telephone 071-831 1772) has a large display of cards advertising cameras for sale.

242 Beware of buying very old items such as baby cots and high chairs which may be coated in paint containing lead. Only if these are at giveaway prices should you consider buying them, as you will have the additional expense of having them stripped and repainted.

243 Never buy any item where the cost of a repair is out of all proportion to the amount you are being asked to pay. Also check whether you can still get spare parts for it.

244 Be wary of buying a secondhand bed – we lose up to one pound of skin and many gallons of moisture per year, much of it when we are in bed. And dust mites in mattresses aggravate asthma or wheezing problems. It's better to wait for the sales and buy a new one. *(See 100.)*

245 For the cost of a secondhand bed you could buy a new Futon. *(See 101.)*

246 People who queue at the doors before jumble sales open, or who are there at the crack of dawn for car boot sales and antique fairs, may get the pick of the items, but not the best bargains. These are to be found just before closing time when unsold items are reduced to rock bottom prices and stall holders are more open to offers.

247 You don't have to be an expert seamstress to run up simple clothes, curtains, duvet covers and other household furnishings. A secondhand sewing machine will recover its cost in no time. Reconditioned sewing machines from major retailers are usually bargains.

Auctions

248   Many antique dealers rely on items bought at auction to stock their shops and so offer the fiercest competition to the private bidder. On the other hand, they have to drop out sooner as their profit margin dwindles. They also have the advantage over most private bidders of experience. But the one thing which seems to be given freely at auctions is advice – from the people running it. They will tell you that the best bargains can often be had in January when people are penniless after Christmas or have been carried away with sales euphoria, and midsummer when many people are away on holiday.

249   Bidding at auction is often made out to be a minefield for the novice and it does pay to have a dry run. Seek out the porters and ask how much an item is likely to fetch and if someone would do the bidding for you. Agree the maximum price you are prepared to pay and allow extra for the porter's tip and the 10% buyer's premium which everyone pays regardless of whether they do their own bidding or not.

250   When you buy the catalogue and go to the preview, inspect the items which interest you very thoroughly and do the same with the rules and conditions of the sale – it will be too late afterwards to discover your mistakes.

251   Electrical and mechanical goods are not a particularly wise buy at auctions as it is difficult to check they are in working order before you buy them.

252   Good buys at auction are job lots of household linen, curtains and rugs that can be cleaned or easily repaired, and, if you have room for them, larger than average pieces of furniture which are too big for the 'modern' home.

253 When bidding for newer items at auction, never go beyond two-thirds of their original shop price.

254 Beware of items like three-piece suites unless they are in impeccable condition, as the cost of recovering them can be almost as much as buying new.

255 When times are hard, luxury items such as cigar humidors, crocodile and pigskin briefcases and handbags, and fairly flashy items of jewellery tend to be more plentiful at auction at a fraction of their original cost. Sellers looking for the best market tend to put them in the pre-Christmas sales.

256 When companies go into liquidation, office furniture can be a good buy at auction. One source is Frank Bowen, 15 Greek Street, London W1V 5LF. Telephone 071-437 3244.

257 *The Daily Telegraph* on Monday, *The Times* on Tuesdays, your local papers and the *Antiques Trade Gazette* are the best sources of information about forthcoming auctions.

258 For a free leaflet on 'Buying and Selling At Auction', contact the Incorporated Society of Auctioneers & Valuers, 3 Cadogan Gate, London SW1X 0AS. Telephone 071-235 2282.

259 London Transport's Lost Property Office at Baker Street Station keeps unclaimed goods for up to three months. Generally only about a third of the items are ever claimed, and the rest are auctioned off monthly by Greasby's of Tooting, 211 Longley Road, London SW17 9LG. Telephone 081-672 1100.

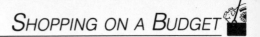

260 Every year thousands of umbrellas, gloves, scarves, hats and other personal belongings are left on British Rail trains. The majority are never claimed. Items are kept for a week or so at the local station, before being sent to the Regional Lost Property Office. If still unclaimed after three months, items are auctioned off, with bargains to be had. Write to Amstey Horne and Co, BR Warehouse, Harrow Road, London W2 for details and a catalogue.

261 Lost Property recovered from the British Airports Authority is sold off by West London Auctions, Sandringham Mews, London W5 on alternate Saturday mornings. The goodies tend to be more upmarket than those left on British Rail – briefcases, suitcases, etc.

Looking Your Best

Buying Clothes and Accessories

 It's easier than ever nowadays to dress well for less, with closing-down sales at every other shop and the boom in charity shops, secondhand and good-as-new boutiques, and dress hire agencies. It also means that if you look after a garment well enough, you may be able to get something back when it's time to trade it in.

 When shopping for secondhand clothes choose smart areas where moneyed people only wear their stylish designer clothes once or twice before passing them on.

264   Take a tip from top dress designer Jean Muir who wears mainly navy and finds it easy to co-ordinate her accessories round this one basic colour which suits her best. Find your most flattering and practical base colour and do the same. You also save on having to take loads of extras when you're on the move. You can always lighten up a dark base colour with brightly coloured scarves and jewellery where it may seem harsh against the face.

265   For cheap casual outdoor wear, try camping centres and Army & Navy Stores. These places stock the same type of reasonably priced items all the year round.

○ **Hats**

266   Choose a classic shaped hat that won't date, in a style which flatters your face and a basic colour which compliments the rest of your wardrobe. You only need one hat, but you can ring the changes with ribbons, scarves, artificial flowers or for a grand occasion, a veil.

○ **Footwear**

267   Secondhand shoes, unless almost new, are not a good buy as they will have moulded themselves to the shape of someone else's feet and will wear unevenly as well as being uncomfortable.

268   Always run a finger round the rims of shoes to check for small rough or knobbly bits which can play havoc with tights and stockings.

269   Long black boots have been an important fashion accessory for certainly as long as most people can remember. Save a small fortune by buying rubber riding boots instead and treating them with leather dressing (available from saddlers). They'll polish to a leather-like shine, but will have the added benefit of being waterproof too.

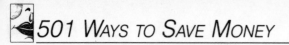

○ *Hosiery*

| 270 | Thrifty dressers buy bargain lots of tights and stockings when the sales are on, avoiding the coloured oddments which you'll probably never wear, and storing up on black or nearly black and flesh tones.

Clothes Care

| 271 | You can often save a trip to the dry cleaners by using safe and gentle fluids and powders which form the basis of more expensive proprietary brands of dry-cleaning aerosols, fluids and dry fabric shampoos. A small phial of petrol – the kind you buy at tobacconists as lighter fuel – is a godsend. Where stain removing remedies mention petrol or benzine, this is the type to use, and Fuller's earth is excellent for delicate materials.

| 272 | Collars on coats usually become grubby before the rest of the garment. Save on dry-cleaning bills by removing grease with a cloth dipped in ammonia. This is suitable for velvet, but hold the garment in front of a hot iron afterwards to draw the pile.

| 273 | Use a little shampoo on dampened cotton wool to clean a hat band, but be sure to follow this with a few drops of vinegar on a clean pad to remove all traces of soap. The other gentler, alternative is to rub the brim with Fuller's earth and leave on overnight to absorb the grease.

| 274 | Delay general wear and tear by never wearing the same shoes and garments more than two days running, if possible. After wearing, brush clothes gently and hang them to air – preferably out of doors. Shine and perspiration marks weaken the material so sponge lightly with a well diluted salt and vinegar solution. Remove perspiration stains with a couple of aspirins dissolved in the water where items are washable.

275 An overwarm washing temperature is often the cause of clothes shrinking or the colours running. Washing in cold water and washing-up liquid or a mild liquid detergent – and always rinsing in water that is the same temperature as the wash water will prevent disasters. If a garment looks a size smaller after washing, gently stretch it to the proper size after removing surplus water by rolling it in a towel. Then leave to dry flat in a well ventilated spot away from direct heat.

276 Haberdashery departments sell suede renovating cloths. They are very expensive and on closer inspection look like very fine sandpaper. Buy very fine grade sandpaper at a fraction of the cost and wrap round a cork block. Clean the suede by rubbing gently in one direction only.

277 There's no need to take garments to the dry cleaners when suede cuffs and collars need renovating. Instead use a soft brush such as a baby's hair brush, dipped in petrol *(see 271)* and rub the worn areas until all the dirt is removed.

278 Where suede handbags have acquired greasy and stained edges, gently rub the affected parts with a fine emery board.

279 Cheap thread is a false economy as it will be forever breaking. Use tough dental floss for sewing buttons on thicker fabrics such as denim. A dab of clear nail varnish on thread once a button has been anchored in place will reinforce its staying power.

○ *Footwear*

280 Saddle soap in glycerine bars, available from saddlers, makes a cheap softener and cleaner for leather shoes and boots.

281 Petroleum jelly is a cheap cleaner and protector for patent leather shoes, lubricating them against cracks and covering scuff marks.

 282 Restore cake shoe polish which has dried out by placing the sealed tin in a shallow bath or boiling water for a few minutes. Remove and mix the polish with a little turpentine.

283 To increase their life, put toe caps and heal guards on everyday shoes while they are still reasonably new.

284 Always ask in advance how much larger shoe repairs will cost. These can come to as much as half of what you paid for the shoes new – especially if they were a sales bargain. Unless you're wildly attached to them, it may be cheaper in the long run to buy new.

○ *Hosiery*

285 Some say that tights and stockings are less likely to snag or ladder, if washed in mild soap suds and left to dry without rinsing. I've also heard that putting wet tights or stockings in a plastic bag in the freezer and thawing and dripping dry before use doubles their life expectancy.

 286 Spraying hairspray on weak points like toes and heels will prolong the life of tights and stockings.

See also 270, 288 and 289.

New Clothes from Old

287 Instead of replacing dingy white underwear which is still sound apart from the colour, re-vamp by dipping in a strong brew of tea or coffee.

288 Boiling tired tights and stockings will produce a potful of neutral coloured ones which can be matched. Boil them together with a dash of washing-up liquid, simmer for ten minutes and rinse.

289 When only one leg of a pair of tights is laddered, cut that leg off at the thigh. When this happens to a second pair in the same colour, you will have two perfectly good legs that can be worn as a pair.

See also 285 and 286.

290 A stained and frayed lining often lets down an otherwise perfectly wearable coat. Revamp it by first unpicking the old lining, pressing it flat and using it as a pattern to cut out a new one. The alternative is to scour the jumble sales for a coat in your size where the nearly new lining is its best feature.

291 Look out for nearly new bargains at jumble sales where the only problem is a broken zip. If the zip fastener has broken near its base it can easily be mended. Pull the slide down until it comes just below the broken teeth, and cut out the damaged part. Pull the slide carefully and evenly to engage the teeth up the two sides. Once past the broken bit, make a new and firm base by stitching across securely.

292 Sometimes items in jumble sales which cost only a few pence are worth buying if the garment has a good set of buttons. Buttons are surprisingly expensive to buy new.

Hairdressing

293 The many hairdressing schools up and down the country constantly require models for students to practise their skills on. The advantage to you is a haircut for little or no cost. Students will be learning basic cutting and styling techniques under expert supervision. You won't, however, be able to choose what you want.

294 Ask at local salons about cheap rates for models. Many salons are more than pleased to give cut-price hairdo's in return for modelling duties. Don't worry if you're not the classic model type – salons have all sorts of clients after all.

295 Many hairdressers offer special prices to students, senior citizens and children – it pays to ask.

296 Despite the exorbitant cost of salon services, we too often accept bad cuts, frizzy perms, and botched colour treatments. Resolve not to any more. Consumer rights under the Supply of Goods and Services Act apply here. If you don't get the result you expected make this known immediately and ask for it to be put right – it would make matters worse to redo the treatment straight away and you may have to wait a few weeks but withhold payment until it is put right. Take photographs and see a doctor if there are any burns – any evidence will be helpful in a dispute. If they aren't sympathetic, or you feel unwilling to let them near your hair again, tell them you will have it put right elsewhere at your own cost and will send them the bill. *(See also 39-41.)*

297 If you can find a freelance hairdresser who visits clients at home, arrange with a group of friends to have a job lot of hairdos at the same time. It should work out relatively cheaply as you will be sharing the hairdresser's transport costs and even the tip. You could try to negotiate on group discount.

298 When limited to an occasional visit to a professional hair-dresser, watch carefully what they do, ask lots of questions and invest in the same type of brushes, setting lotions or styling aids. Explain to the stylist that you want a cut or perm which will be easy to look after.

See also 231.

Hair Care

○ *Shampoos and conditioners*

299 Adding a teaspoon of powdered starch to your ordinary shampoo will help greasy hair to go longer between washes.

|300| Talcum powder makes an effective dry shampoo. Your hairbrush, with a nylon stocking pulled over it, will collect surplus grease. Be sure to remove every trace of powder so that it won't clog the scalp.

|301| Eggs have been a popular ingredient in hair shampoos and conditioners for many years. Make a nourishing but inexpensive treatment for dry and brittle hair by mixing one egg with a tablespoon of cider vinegar or lemon juice and beating together until light and fluffy. Apply to the hair after shampooing and leave on for 15 minutes. Rinse carefully with warm not hot water or the egg will scramble.

|302| For a cheap conditioner for dry and split ends, massage a tablespoon of homemade mayonnaise into the ends. Cover with a warm towel and let the mayonnaise penetrate the hair for 30 minutes before shampooing off.

|303| For a scalp treatment and conditioner mix together 2 tablespoons of olive oil, 1 teaspoon of lemon juice or vinegar, and 2 teaspoons of honey. Massage in, leave for 30 minutes then rinse out and shampoo in the usual way.

○ *Setting lotion*

|304| Beer makes an excellent setting lotion, giving terrific body to the hair. And toilet water or eau de cologne will give a quick set to any locks, but will be particularly effective on greasy hair that needs a lift, as they have a drying effect.

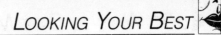

○ *Highlights and colour enhancing*

305 Highlights are expensive as a salon treatment. Instead, accelerate the sun's natural bleaching process by rubbing neat lemon juice on hair with a pad of cotton wool. Let it dry in the sun for natural looking highlights. Be sure to follow with a conditioner to counteract any drying effect the treatment may have.

306 When washing your hair add a little wine vinegar to the rinsing water to remove all traces of shampoo and give a shine to any colour hair, but in particular brown hair.

307 An infusion of walnut leaves (a handful of leaves boiled up in a pint of water and applied when cool) will bring out the best in chestnut hair. Use the same method but substitute sage leaves for grey hair to make it darker, and substitute chamomile for fair hair.

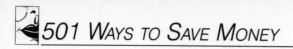

Beauty Treatments

○ *Face*

 For dry and sensitive skins, mix a few drops of almond oil into the yolk of an egg and thin down with a few drops of fresh lemon or orange juice. Apply all over the face and neck, avoiding the eye area. Remove after 15 minutes.

309 An effective face mask for a really greasy skin can be made by mixing a lightly beaten egg white with 2 teaspoons of cornflour. Apply all over the face and neck, avoiding the eye area, and leave to dry. When you feel your skin becoming taut, wait one more minute then rinse off and pat dry.

310 Dissolve a heaped tablespoon of borax in half a cup of warm water and, using cotton wool, dab on round the nose and chin for an effective treatment for open pores.

311 Leftover egg white on its own or mixed with oatmeal, can be left on the centre panel of the face as a treatment mask for open pores.

○ *Eyes and lashes*

 When not due to ill health or too many late nights, puffy eyes can be caused by getting heavy face cream near the eye area. So be careful when applying cream, particularly at night. Proprietary remedies are expensive, but plain ice-cold water compresses, slices of cucumber, raw potato, or chilled used tea bags all do a good job of soothing tired eyes and reducing puffiness and bags.

313 You can make your own cheap but effective eye mask by mixing equal quantities of rosewater and witch hazel. Store in a bottle and apply on strips of bandage.

314 Petroleum jelly is an indispensable security aid for those on a tight budget. It removes mascara while at the same time promoting a thick growth of lashes. And a good tip to prevent lashes breaking when using an eyelash curler is to smear a little petroleum jelly on to the inside rims of the curler. *(See also 325.)*

315 Before getting into the bath, smear a little castor oil round the eye area to soften wrinkles and feed lashes as you soak. Blot off the excess as you dry yourself.

See also 346 and 347.

○ **Baths**

316 A few drops of sunflower oil added to the bath is about the cheapest body and water softener around.

317 Make your own heated bath pillow by filling a hot water bottle with warm water before you get in the bath for a good soak. The gentle heat will relax the muscles of your neck and shoulders as well as providing a perfectly good head rest.

○ **Hands, feet and nails**

318 A plastic washing-up bowl of hot water in which you have dissolved a handful of Epsom salts may not look as elegant as the posh foot spas you can buy, but it will draw out all the pain and relax the muscles of tired feet just as well. Following the soak with a soothing foot massage using warm olive oil. Do this once a week if you can.

For a do-it-yourself manicure, soak the fingertips in a cup of warm water with a tablespoon of bicarbonate of soda dissolved in it. This will bleach and strengthen the nails and can be followed, after patting dry, with a soak in warm olive oil to condition them and promote growth.

 Acetone (available from chemists) is the cheapest type of nail varnish remover, but it is too harsh unless you add a few drops of castor oil to the bottle and shake well before each use.

 Colourless nail varnish is the most practical and economical type to buy. It doesn't need replacing quite so often and does many other jobs, from stopping ladders in tights to reinforcing sewing threads on buttons *(see 279)*.

 Nail varnish often becomes too thick to apply evenly when the bottle is nowhere near empty. To remedy this, add a few drops of nail varnish remover to the bottle, stand it for a few minutes in boiling water then give it a good shake. Keeping it in the fridge will stop it clogging and give you miles more coverage. It will also dry more quickly when applied to the nails.

Make-up

 No need to buy lip pencils as well as lipstick. Instead invest in a lip brush and use to give a professional outline to lips. Lipstick applied with a brush will last longer on the lips, and you'll be able to use up every trace of lipstick right down to the bottom of the bare stub.

 No need to buy blusher as well as lipstick. Put a trace of lipstick in the palm of your hand and add a drop of foundation. Mix together and blend over cheekbones.

Save on buying lip gloss and lip salve by simply using petroleum jelly. It will give a glossy look to lips and at the same time protect them from chapping.

326 Make-up brushes can be expensive, but you'll find a wide variety of suitable inexpensive brushes at art shops. Wash them well before using for the first time, and let them sit for a minute in fabric or hair conditioner to make them extra soft.

327 Mascara often dries out in its container making it impossible to use. Instead of throwing away, screw the lid on tightly and immerse in hot water for a few minutes. You'll be able to squeeze the last drops from a tube of cream, foundation or toothpaste by using this method.

328 Instead of the more expensive coloured tissues, buy tough man-sized tissues and only use half a one at a time. Or use a soft loo roll for economy.

See also 332 and 333.

Note
Homemade beauty products have a naturally limited shelf life, but most should last for up to 2 weeks if kept in the fridge.

Health and First Aid

Medicines and Dressings

 329 Look for BP (British Pharmacopoeia) or BPC (British Pharmaceutical Codex) standard brand products when buying medicines. They are nearly always cheaper than the proprietary brands.

330 Some medicines are actually cheaper when bought over the counter than on prescription at the dispensary. Hydrocortisone cream is one example. You can't rely on your doctor to point out these savings, and some will routinely hand out NHS prescriptions to NHS patients. It's worth asking your GP before you leave, or the pharmacist at the dispensing chemist, before you hand over the money.

331 It's more economical to buy plasters in a strip or on a roll than boxes of individual precut shapes.

332 Cotton wool rolls or pleats are more economical than bags of cotton wool balls, and surgical wool is cheapest of all.

333 Get twice as much cotton wool for your money by buying bumper packs of surgical wool, unrolling this and leaving in a warm airing cupboard or on top of a radiator until the heat makes it swell to nearly double its size. Cut into strips for convenient use.

First Aid

○ *Sores, spots and stings*

334 For some reason black coffee can rapidly dispel cold sores. Apply neat every 2 or 3 hours and leave to dry. Alternatively try a drop of perfume.

335 Instead of buying yet another brand of spot cream, cover the latest eruption with a dab of toothpaste. Or a rub with the cut side of half an onion or lemon. These are age-old correctives, but they do sting.

336 For recurring spots invest in a styptic pencil (available at chemists) which is more commonly used to stop bleeding. It's convenient to carry around and works well for regular use.

337 A safe and soothing balm for mild rashes and dry skin disorders can be made by mixing equal quantities of soft white paraffin and liquid paraffin.

Citronella oil, available from chemists, is much cheaper than many brands of insect repellant. It can also be applied directly to bites to soothe them. Take a small plastic bottle to the chemist and ask them to fill it for you.

 Toothpaste is a less conventional sting reliever for mosquito bites, while bicarbonate of soda mixed to a paste with a little water works for bee stings, and neat vinegar for wasp stings.

○ **Mouth and throat**

340 To soothe and heal a mouth ulcer add a good pinch of bicarbonate of soda to half a tumbler of warm water and gargle well. Dab dry and apply toothpaste to the ulcer or a drop of neat whisky.

341 Don't spend money on proprietary mouthwashes. Add a few drops of vinegar to a tumbler of water and swill round the mouth. The vinegar acts as a cleanser, deodoriser and mild antiseptic, so is particularly useful as a mouthwash for bleeding or ulcerated gums.

 Instead of buying breath freshener capsules, chew fresh parsley, cardamom seeds, cloves or coffee beans. Alternatively, chew a slice of lemon – skin, pith, pips and all.

343 To relieve a sore throat, gargle with soluble aspirin dissolved in water and drink copious amounts of warm water generously laced with lemon juice and honey. Don't use boiling water as it will destroy valuable vitamin C in the lemon juice.

○ *Indigestion and hangovers*

344 Indigestion powders and tablets can be cheaply and effectively replaced with a cupful of boiled water or a few teaspoons of neat lemon juice sipped slowly.

345 Proprietary hangover remedies are often nothing more than antacid tablets. You will get just as much benefit by adding a pinch of bicarbonate of soda to a glass of warm water and sipping it slowly. If the hangover is really severe, take a couple of soluble aspirins and drink masses of water.

○ *Eye care*

346 Eye lotions are expensive to buy and once the bottle has been opened it should not be kept for long. Save money and make your own as and when you need it. Dissolve a teaspoon of bicarbonate of soda in a pint (600ml) of warm water that has previously been boiled. Use to bath tired or itchy eyes.

347 For instant relief for eyes which are red and inflamed, splash with ice cold water.

See also 312-315.

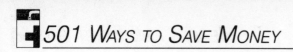

Cheaper Specs

348 In 1989 a change in the law meant that free sight tests were abolished for all but 38% of the population (children, students, those on low incomes, diabetics and glaucoma sufferers). At the same time the Government allowed the sale of ready-to-wear reading glasses without a prescription. It is foolish to try to save money by neglecting regular eye tests, but really substantial savings can be made when buying reading glasses as I discovered when I set out to buy the cheapest and best with the shortest waiting time. After paying for my sight test, I took my prescription to the Headquarters of Crown Eyeglass, Britain's biggest manufacturers of ready-to-wear spectacles, at Blackburn in Lancashire. They made my prescription lenses (including a tint) in exactly four minutes. It took me a little longer to choose frames – almost identical to the designer ones I'd fancied at a smart opticians – and I saved over half the cost of the prices I'd been quoted in the High Street. So it really does pay to shop around.

349 When you need new glasses, consider having new lenses put in your existing frames. New frames are expensive and can easily cost more than the lenses.

Dental Care

350 Some dental patients who think they are getting NHS treatment can be floored by bills for private care. Check exactly what you will have to pay for and whether you may be eligible for free treatment at the time you arrange an appointment. And remember that if you cancel an appointment without giving the required notice, a dentist can charge for loss of time.

351 To remove stains from dentures or dingy teeth, rub with bicarbonate of soda on a dry toothbrush.

352 Following teeth cleaning sessions with a pinch of salt in the rinsing water keeps teeth bright and the mouth fresh.

Entertaining on a Shoestring

Ideas

 When entertaining it's worth remembering that it isn't the food or the drink you serve so much as how you present it that counts. A crusty apple pie in a lovely dish might well be made with windfalls, for example. Final touches like pretty tables, napkins and flowers, and jugs of soft drinks decorated with sprigs of mint and slices of fruit for those who don't drink alcohol are always welcomed. In fact your attention to guests' needs will be remembered long after the food they ate or the drink on offer are forgotten.

354 The American idea of a 'brunch' party lends itself to less elaborate food based on bread, muffins, fruit, eggs and economical dishes like kedgeree. Most people drink less mid morning than at night, and some cheap sparkling wine mixed with orange juice for a poor man's bucks fizz, and coffee or iced tea, all make ideal accompaniments.

355 Summertime entertaining always has the added possibility of eating 'al fresco' and you don't need even a garden. Invite friends for a picnic and choose a location (there are many ideas for outings in free leaflets available from your local tourist office). If you're near a river, how about a boat trip? Membership of zoological societies often carries concessionary rates for yourself, family and friends and is ideal for entertaining children. Picnic food needn't be expensive or boring. Interesting salads, pâtés, crusty French bread, a few nice cheeses and fresh fruit, plus plenty of chilled drinks if the weather is hot, won't stretch the budget too badly but will go down a treat.

356 With your closest friends, who could well be in the same financial boat as you, you may be able to suggest a joint entertaining venture. You could offer to provide a main course, if someone else brings the starter and another makes the pud, salads and cheeses, etc.

357 If you have a garden an excellent way of entertaining is to tell your guests you are providing a barbecue with salads and other accompaniments and you would like them to bring their own meat or fish to cook on the fire. The other advantage of this apart from cutting the cost of the priciest food item, is that if friends bring other friends or family you don't have to go into your loaves and fishes act of feeding the 5,000 from 6 hamburgers and a pound of sausages.

358   It's nice to be able to entertain by having people to stay. The main requirement is something comfortable to sleep on. If you don't have a spare bed buy a Futon for a fraction of the price. Another advantage of a Futon is that it can be rolled up and stored away when space is needed. You'll also need to provide guests with a place to hang clothes. This could be a simple concertina-style wooden clothes horse with a few coat hangers on it. A table with a good reading light, some reading material, a jug of water and a tumbler, and fresh towels are the only other things you need, a few flowers next to the bedside make a nice touch – especially if they are from the garden.

359   One of the cheapest and prettiest ideas for floral decoration without using much in the way of bought flowers is to fill an attractive bowl with water and lay in it small shoots with fresh green and variegated leaves, clusters of berries and flower heads. When there's honeysuckle on the hedgerows and other wild flowers in abundance in spring and summer this needn't cost you a penny and being so close to the water the flowers stay fresher longer.

Drink

360   Homemade wine and beer is cheaper than the bought variety, but the quality will depend on the skill of the winemaker and the quality of the kit. You will also need to invest in certain items of equipment. Before going ahead it pays to study books on the subject, such as those in the Amateur Wine Maker series.

361   If ordering drinks for a party from an off-licence or wine-merchant, ask for them on a 'use or return basis'. That way you needn't be frightened of buying too many bottles as you will be able to return the unopened ones.

362 When buying wine in quantity, it usually works out cheaper if bought by the case rather than individually. Many wine merchants will let you put a mixed case together.

363 Don't give guests choices of alcoholic drinks. Stick to wine, sherry, or a punch for example. If having wine, however, do have red and white on offer as many people have a distinct preference. It's likely that one will be more popular than the other so make sure you have an adequate supply of both kinds. *(See 361.)*

364 The wine merchant you buy your drinks from may be able to let you have glasses for free at the same time. You will, of course, have to pay for any you break.

365 Supermarket offers on wine are very tempting and often beat the small wine merchant hands down. It's better to buy a good wine at a reduced price than to buy cheap plonk. Try to budget so you can buy the odd bargain bottle to put away for entertaining.

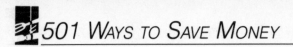

366 Dress up inexpensive wines to make a little go a long way by having sangria parties in summer or serving mulled wine with homemade mince pies at Christmas.

367 If you get through a lot of soft drinks, invest in a soda syphon kit and make your own fizzy drinks for a fraction of the usual price.

368 In an emergency where that half empty bottle of tonic has gone deadly flat, drop a pinch of bicarbonate of soda in it and give it a gentle shake. No one will know the difference.

369 If you have half an orange or lemon in the fridge, before it goes off slice and freeze it on its own or place in ice cubes trays, cover with water and freeze to make attractive ice cubes for drinks.

370 You don't have to buy extra ice cube trays for parties. Instead use the bottom half of plastic egg boxes filled with water. As they freeze pop them in a plastic bag in the freezer to collect a big batch. A quick squirt with a soda syphon soon separates ice cubes that have stuck together.

371 You will, inevitably, have leftover opened bottles of wine after a party. If you intend to use it up in cooking, it will keep for much longer if you add a few drops of olive oil to the bottle. Alternatively, white wine leftovers can be added to a bottle of vinegar.

Food

○ *Party nibbles*

372 Dips are a good means of filling people up and make a change from nuts and crisps. Eke out the main ingredients with yoghurt or soured cream and serve with sticks of celery, carrots, cauliflower florets, etc.

373 The following dip is inexpensive to make and can be prepared the day before. Mash 4oz (100g) tuna fish and blend in 8oz (225g) cream cheese followed by ½pint (300ml) soured cream or yoghurt. Add a large clove of crushed garlic and a few drops of tabasco sauce. Season to taste.

374 Look out for cut-price Stilton, Danish Blue or similar cheeses. They are often greatly reduced after Christmas. Keep them in the freezer until you have a drinks party. Allow to thaw out then mash with butter or margarine and use to fill the hollows of celery sticks. Chill and cut into bite-sized pieces before serving.

375 Inexpensive toppings for canapes include sliced hardboiled eggs on top of homemade anchovy butter; lumpfish roe on soft cheese; and chicken liver pâté, kipper pâté (*see 390*) and sliced smoked mackerel on a bed of soured cream.

376 Where serving salted peanuts jazz them up and make them taste like those expensive packets from delicatessens. Heat a knob of butter in a pan, until frothy, add 2 teaspoons of curry powder and cook for a minute. Add the nuts and fry them in the spicy mix for a further 2 minutes. Drain them on a piece of absorbent paper and leave to cool.

○ *Roasts*

377 Always put meat on a rack in the roasting tin, this stops the base from becoming overcooked and gives you an extra portion when you carve.

378 Always roast a chicken upside down so that the juices run into the breast and the meat will, by staying moist, go much further.

○ **Minced meat**

 One day I think I shall write a book called *A Thousand and One Things to Do with Mince!* It is so useful when providing meals for large numbers of people and can be turned into dozens of tasty, inexpensive dishes from hamburgers to lasagne, moussaka to curry, and cottage pie to chili con carne or spaghetti bolognese. What's more a little can be eked out to feed a lot. Look for cut-price offers in the shops or, better still, invest in a mincer so that you can buy the cheaper cuts of meat, like neck and shin, which usually need long slow cooking, but once minced they cook quickly and make thrifty, tasty dishes.

 Use oatmeal to thicken mince dishes instead of flour, to make the dish go further.

 Meat balls with spicy tomato sauce are useful as a buffet table dish or they can be made mini size for drinks parties.

 When making hamburgers add a few tablespoons of fresh breadcrumbs to the meat after you've watered the mince with 4fl ozs (100ml) of water per 1lb (450g) and you'll get at least one extra portion out of the mixture.

 Mix mince with sausage meat and/or mushrooms to stretch a meat loaf – or add an individual serving sized box of Rice Krispies to give it a lighter texture.

Any leftover mince can be seasoned with the addition of a few fresh herbs or a dash of Tabasco or Worcestershire Sauce, then used to stuff mushrooms, courgettes and other vegetables, or pancakes which are also easy and cheap to make.

○ *General*

Consider serving a pasta dish when entertaining for large numbers. It's not only economical and versatile but is filling too, and only needs a simple salad as an accompaniment.

If you add a couple of drops of yellow food colouring to bought noodles you can pretend they are the fresh homemade variety and impress your guests.

387

Whipped double cream will go further if yoghurt or whipped egg white is folded into it – and it'll be less fattening and more healthy for your guests.

388

When making batches of sandwiches for a tea party or picnic make the butter go much further and spread more easily by beating half a teacup of lukewarm milk into each half pound (225g) of butter.

389 A batch of pancakes is cheap to make and can be prepared in advance and kept separated by greaseproof paper. They can even be frozen. For a quick dessert place a tablespoon of ice cream in the centre of each, fold in half and pour over a hot fruit sauce.

390 Here's a cheap starter to serve four which tastes like it's an expensive fish such as smoked trout. It is in fact the humble kipper, cunningly disguised. Fillet 2 large fat juicy kippers into four pieces. Place 2 fillets side by side in the bottom of a smallish deep china dish with tightly fitting lid. Sprinkle enough chopped Spanish onion over them to cover. Put the other 2 kipper fillets on top and cover with olive oil. Leave the covered fish in the bottom of the fridge to marinate for at least a fortnight, longer is better – up to two months. Serve, well drained, with brown bread and butter, and say not a word about the origins of this delicious smoked fish delicacy.

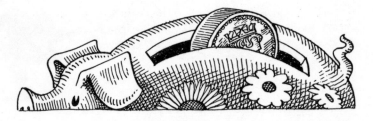

Miles Further on Motoring Expenses

Car Maintenance

391 A cut onion rubbed on the windscreen will stop it freezing over. A dash of methylated spirits in the windscreen water bottle is cheaper than using antifreeze.

392 Keep newspapers in the car to lay over the windscreen and stop it freezing. Hold in place with the wipers or tape on with waterproof tape, which is also useful for taping over the locks to avoid freezing.

393 Don't buy bottled distilled water for batteries when you can save the water from a defrosted fridge to top them up.

394   Brasso will rub light scratches off car paint.

395   Where scratches and chips on the bodywork are too deeply ingrained to be rubbed off by Brasso, a child's wax crayon in a matching colour will act as a filler and stop the rust getting in.

396   To remove corrosion from car batteries, use a dense solution of bicarbonate of soda in water and apply with a toothbrush. Leave until dry, then remove with a steel brush or wire wool. When dry, smear the terminal caps with petroleum jelly.

397   It pays to tackle the smallest rust spots on bodywork as they appear. Apply olive or linseed oil to the rust for several days before rubbing down with fine steel wool or an emery board.

398   To prevent rust on chrome, coat with a thin protective film of linseed oil or petroleum jelly after each car wash.

399   Albert Tyler, who has for many years run car maintenance courses, says that 'By far the largest proportion of car break-down problems – say 80%-90% – are caused by simple little faults left to develop into major problems or created by lack of simple maintenance and inspection procedures which anyone can, and should carry out in minutes at regular intervals. He has writen a smashing inexpensive booklet which is crammed with super tips on maintenance and driving and should save you a small fortune. *Car Sense* costs £2.50 plus 45p postage and packing, and is available from Tyler Publications, 2 Glynderwen Close, Sketty, Swansea, West Glamorgan, Wales SA2 8EQ. Telephone: (0792) 203213.

400   Get into the habit of regularly checking fluid indicators for the radiator, battery, engine oil, brake and clutch reservoirs. A noticeable drop can alert you in time to see to it immediately, avoiding a potentially larger bill for repairs if you do nothing about it.

401 Apart from the obvious safety element, checking tyre pressures regularly can help save fuel as a higher pressure reduces the rolling resistance of the tyre, which in turn lowers fuel consumption. Keep to the car manufacturers' recommended pressures – too high or too low is dangerous.

402 Choose a garage which is AA or RAC approved or covered by a code of practice laid down by their trade association. If you are not happy with a service or repairs, put your complaint in writing to the garage manager and send a copy to your local Trading Standards Office, the consumer affairs adviser at your local Citizens Advice Bureau or the AA, RAC or relevant trade association depending on the signs or logos displayed at the garage.

403 Get a written quote for a major job including VAT labour and parts. Ask them to contact you to get your permission to exceed the figure before they carry on, and ask for a detailed invoice to be ready at the time you collect the vehicle.

○ *Servicing and repairs*

404 Although it makes sense while a car is still under warranty to use only approved agents to carry out servicing and repairs, once the warranty has expired you should compare the prices of local garages and get personal recommendations if possible.

405 Cars which develop rattles and squeaks rarely reproduce them to order when you want to impress a mechanic. Record the sound on a portable audio cassette as you drive and play it back at the garage. Saves labour charges and your petrol as they cruise around the countryside waiting for sound of impending disaster to be heard above the blare of your radio.

Fuel Economy

406 The drivers' right foot is the best economy device a car has, say the AA. They recommend that you avoid fast getaways and sudden braking – you use 60% more fuel with a racing start rather than a slow smooth one.

407 Where practical, use the highest gear you can to maintain speeds, cruising when possible. Lower gears use up to 50% more petrol – the highest fuel consumption is in low-gear, low-speed traffic, so get into top gear as soon as the engine is ready.

408 Avoid accelerating up to traffic lights, obstructions and T-junctions and braking sharply.

409   Keeping the choke out for too long after a cold start not only uses a lot of petrol but washes away the protective oil film on cylinder walls and so wears the engine unduly.

410   Shop around for petrol – even a few pence different per litre each time you fill up can amount to a significant sum over a year. Find out the best deals from tyre specialists rather than allowing garages to replace them when the car is in for a service or pre MOT check. The tyres will be more expensive at the garage.

Buying and Selling a Car

411   The best time to sell your car is when buyers come out of winter hibernation in the spring, and the worst time is after the new registration appears on 1st August when the number of secondhand cars for sale increases – making it a good time to buy a secondhand car.

412   Cars generally become costly to keep, needing major repairs when 4-6 years old with a mileage of between 40,000 and 60,000. It is a good time to sell your car when it gets to this stage.

413   Before selling a car, get an idea of its value from ads in local papers or car price guides. You will then avoid selling the car too cheaply, as well as pricing yourself out of the market.

414   You will be better off selling privately as a dealer will generally offer less, even when you are trading in for a new model.

415   When selling privately it is standard practice to wait until the buyer's cheque has cleared before handing over the car and vehicle registration document. Otherwise specify payment by a banker's draft.

416 The greatest depreciation in used cars comes in the first two years – their value can drop by at least a third, so the best bargains for secondhand buyers can be found here. A motoring magazine will give you a guide as to which makes and models hold their value best. Big bargains can also be had in 'nearly new' demonstration cars.

417 It's wise when buying a secondhand car to take along a friendly mechanic or ask the AA or RAC to conduct an independent inspection of the vehicle. You must join the AA on top of the inspection fee, but the RAC will make inspection visits for non members, although these are charged at a higher rate. If a seller objects to this type of survey, don't think of buying from him. If he's agreeable he might be persuaded to knock half the inspection fee off the price.

418 If you leave a deposit, ask for 'subject to inspection' to be written on the receipt. That way you will get your deposit back if it fails a later inspection.

419 If you do your own inspection of a secondhand car, go over the bodywork with a magnet which won't react to bodyfiller so you can detect any cunningly disguised dents, cracks or holes in the bodywork.

420 Another test you can do yourself is to hold a rag over the exhaust pipe and ask the seller to start the engine. After a few seconds inspect the rag to see how much oil has stained it. More than a few specks spells trouble.

421 Always ask to see the vehicle registration document, its service record and, if the car is more than 3 years old, its MOT certificate. On no account touch a car which hasn't got the necessary documentation.

422 When buying from a dealer you will be able to find out the previous owner's name and address from the vehicle registration document. If possible ask them about the car's history and check whether the mileage is correct.

423 Dealers will usually offer credit terms to buyers but you could get better rates from a personal bank loan. It pays to investigate the cheapest method.

See also 34-37.

Holidays and Travel

Coach Travel

 Coach travel usually works out cheaper than rail and is often far more comfortable. Your travel agent and local bus company will have details of current offers.

 National Express is Britain's biggest company with daily services to some 1,500 destinations in England and Wales and, through Caledonian Express, to Scotland. With a special discount card a discount of around 30% is available to those over 60, young people between 16 and 23 and students in full time education. Visitors to Britain and group bookings also qualify for lower prices.

British Rail and London Underground

426 Buy a one-day travelcard when journeying into or around London by bus, underground or BR if you are likely to make several journeys. Children under five travel free with a cut-price child fare for 5 to 15 year olds.

427 British Rail offer special discounts to pensioners, students and families. The Senior Citizens' Railcard entitles the holder to at least a third off most fares (the bigger discounts apply to off-peak times).

428 Anyone under 24 – or any mature student in full-time education – should consider a Young Persons' Railcard which entitles you to a third off the standard fare including cheap day returns and savers.

429 Anyone under 26 can obtain an Inter Rail Ticket for up to one months' unlimited travel in 22 European countries with additional discounts to be had en route. Pick up a brochure and tickets from any BR travel centre.

430 The Family Railcard, which is available to anyone over 18, allows adults half or a third off standard class travel when accompanied by up to four children (under 16) who only pay £1. The adults and children don't have to be related, but there must always be at least one child travelling with an adult named on the railcard. This card cannot be used to buy first class tickets.

431 The Disabled Person's Railcard entitles the holder to between a third and a half off specified fares. Enquire at your local station about the qualifications, but the concession also applies to any person required to accompany a severely disabled passenger.

432 A BR Network Card is only valid in the Network South East area, but that extends as far West as Exeter and as far North as King's Lynn. You can save a third on normal-priced adult fare for the holder and up to 3 accompanying adults plus up to four children (aged 5-15) who pay a flat rate of £1. Two adults can be named as holders on the same card – which can be used any time on Saturdays, Sundays and Bank Holidays, but permitted travel times are restricted to off peak hours on weekdays. Ask about a Network Gold Card which has additional concessions for Annual Season Ticket holders and London (bus and tube) Travelcard holders.

433 There is usually ample warning before rail fares rise. You get best value for money if you buy your season ticket just prior to the increase, and if you get it to cover as long a period as possible. So it could work out cheaper to renew before your existing season ticket expires.

434 It pays to enquire at local travel centres about Inter City Savers and other cheap fares or special offers. And if you only want to make an outward journey check whether it is in fact cheaper to buy a return ticket. Curiously a return ticket is often less than half the standard fare.

435 A 25% discount is given to any group of at least ten people travelling together (16 or 17 year olds within the group are allowed a child fare less 25%).

436 If you are going on a long train journey, particularly if it's at peak time, treat yourself to a reserved seat. It's only a little extra on top of your ticket and carries on to the second train should you have to change trains in the course of your journey. It's also worth taking your own food and drink with you and avoiding the high priced traveller's fare refreshments – and the queue to get them.

Air Travel

437 Some airlines deliberately overbook their flights, assuming that several passengers will not turn up. The best policy is to get there early. If you can't get a seat on a flight you've booked, despite what they may tell you to the contrary, the airline *is* in breach of contract and may have to pay compensation. If, however, they offer to get you to your destination within so many hours in lieu of a refund, and you accept, you will probably lose further legal rights.

438 Airlines do not have to pay compensation if your holiday is delayed by a strike, adverse weather conditions or any other reason beyond their control. If, however, the delay could have been avoided, the airline at fault must compensate you with overnight hotel expenses, meals etc., as appropriate. Take the matter up with the customer relations officer, or ultimately the airline chief executive if fair compensation is refused.

439 Most airlines are happy to provide games, colouring materials and other more essential items for children such as baby food, nappies and cots. This not only saves you money, but cuts down on hand baggage. Contact the airline beforehand to find out what's available and don't be afraid to ask for supplies once on board.

440 There is a statute limitation on how much you can claim from an airline which is why you should take out your own insurance cover beforehand. But you can pay an excess value charge at the check in desk to cover valuable items. If your luggage is damaged in transit, show it to officials on the spot and complain in writing as soon as possible.

441 When looking for bargain flights you can't do better than to contact the Air Travel Advisory Bureau who co-ordinate information from travel agents throughout the country. They don't sell holidays or tickets but tell you who to ring to get the best deals. They also advise on visas, insurance, car hire etc., and supply useful fact sheets on your destination. This is a super service and it's absolutely free. Air Travel Advisory Bureau, 41-45 Goswell Road, London EC1V 7DN. Telephone: 071-636 5000 or 071-436 6016.

442 If you are travelling independently it can often work out cheaper than the standard fare if you buy a one-way ticket here and the ticket for your homeward journey abroad.

Cheaper Holidays

|443| Holidaymakers are now generally conditioned to accept that 'package' holidays offer cheaper rates than those available to the independent traveller. This is certainly not always the case. It often pays to get all the brochures available and ring or write to the hotels yourself. Often such friendly personal exchanges can result in special deals, with surcharges for single people and balconies with sea view etc, being waived. Do make sure you get confirmation in writing of what you've agreed, and remember to take this with you on the journey.

|444| Anyone who has ever had the maddening experience of meeting inmates of the hotel enjoying the same meals and hotel facilities but for less money than you paid, has found out about last minute bargains the hard way. You have maximum choice and peace of mind by booking your package holiday months ahead, but spectacular discounts can often be had if you wait and book at the last minute, taking advantage of underfilled flights and hotels, and cancellations.

|445| If you pay for a holiday costing over £100 with a credit card you will automatically get protection should the holiday company go out of business. You must ensure, however, that the credit card voucher is made out to the tour operator and not the travel agent. If a travel agent refuses to do this, go to another who will.

|446| It makes sense to choose a travel agent who is a member of ABTA as they will be governed by ABTA's code of conduct and you will have the backing of ABTA should you have a complaint.

Association of British Travel Agents (ABTA),
55-57 Newman Street,
London W1P 4AH.
Telephone: 071-637 2444.

447 If you feel you have a justifiable complaint about your holiday then collect as much evidence as you can to substantiate your allegations – photographs, names and addresses of fellow travellers who would support you, personnel to whom you previously registered dissatisfaction, etc. You would be surprised how often a well mannered protest about bad service is compensated with a discount on your next holiday or even a complimentary ticket.

448 One of the cheapest ways to have a family holiday is house swapping. This also solves the problem of what to do with pets, plants etc. Your bank will take care of personal documents, precious items of jewellery and other valuables. Intervac, Britain's largest houseswap agency includes many overseas homes. Telephone: 0332 558 931.

449 If you simply can't afford to go away, but yearn for a break, try house sitting a friend's place while they go away, on the basis that they will do the same for you one day. If they're going away for any length of time, choose a friend with an easily maintained garden. The real joy is that very few people need know you're there and the change will do you good.

450 Money-saving holidays for single parent families can be arranged through Gingerbread, the Association for One Parent Families. They keep a register of members offering accommodation on an exchange basis. Cruse (The National Association for the Widowed and their children) is well worth contacting for holiday information, if you are widowed with children. Write enclosing a stamped addressed envelope, to: Gingerbread, Association for One Parent Families, 35 Wellington Street, London WC2. Cruse, 126 Sheen Road, Richmond, Surrey.

451 You don't have to be below a certain age to take advantage of the inexpensive but excellent accommodation offered by the Youth Hostelling Association. Hostels are graded from the basic to the fairly luxurious and it's a very matey system so be prepared to share a room (except out of season). Very reasonably priced meals can be provided if you don't want to cook. Details of membership, locations and rates are available from The Youth Hostels' Association (England and Wales), 29 John Adam Street, London WC2. Telephone: 071-839 1722.

○   *Car hire*

452 In some countries where labour is comparatively cheap, it's often scarcely more expensive to hire a car complete with driver than to hire one without – and that way you'll probably get a more reliable car.

Holiday Homes

453 Beware a Timeshare Tout bearing gifts! Make it an absolute rule never to be badgered into a commitment during your holiday. And never hand over a deposit on the spot simply to qualify for a 'once only' discount or other tempting offers. If you are interested, wait until you return home and consult a solicitor who specialises in overseas property. (Look in *The Solicitor's Regional Directory* or contact The Law Society – *see 39 and 40*.)

454 If you really are keen on the idea of a share in a permanent holiday home, clubbing together with other enterprising friends to form a syndicate scheme to buy a property could prove a shrewd investment. You would have control of maintenance costs – one of the biggest complaints about timeshare developments – and by letting it in the weeks when no one else wants to go, you could cover the cost of your own holidays.

455 Before deciding to retire or buy a holiday home in foreign parts, go and live there for a few months out of season. The advantages of this in money saving terms are two fold; you will prevent an enormously expensive mistake if it turns out to be far less idyllic than on a shorter holiday visit, by going in winter you get rock-bottom longterm rates from hotels and airlines, and what you save on home fuel bills and other pricey winter essentials in Britain will pay for your keep while out there.

Holiday Money

|456| Travellers cheques are gradually being given the heave-ho in favour of Eurocheque cards. These allow you to use your ordinary cheque book when abroad. The advantages of a Eurocheque card is that the money is not debited from your account until after you write the cheque, whereas with travellers' cheques the bank has your money before you cash the cheques. A Eurocheque card has to be ordered in advance. Most banks make a charge, so do shop around as the rates and restrictions can vary enormously.

|457| Where you must use travellers' cheques you will invariably get a better rate at the local banks than at your hotel. It's worth shopping around too – a small bank situated in a side street will more than likely offer better rates than a bank situated on a busy main street. The queues will probably be shorter too.

Shopping

○ *Duty frees*

|458| Duty free goods are generally cheaper and the choice greater in airport lounges rather than on the plane. In Mediterranean countries wine is cheaper in local supermarkets, but spirits are nearly always a better buy at the airport. It's worth remembering that alcohol allowances are more generous if you buy from local shops rather than at the airport in EC countries. When comparing prices, check the quantities marked on the label. Alcohol, for example, is usually sold in 70 or 75cl bottles in foreign supermarkets, but in litre sizes at airports.

459 Perfume is cheaper on the return ferry from France, oddly enough, than it is in France – the country where you might expect the biggest bargains. But cigarettes are a better buy in a French supermarket than en route, and smokers get the best buys in Greece and the Canary Islands where cigarettes are particularly cheap.

460 If you spread the load over a family you can get extra in the way of cheaper gifts – Children under 17 years can bring in perfume and toilet water, but not alcohol or cigarettes.

461 With holidays in Florida and other parts of the US becoming increasingly popular, it pays to note that you must buy airport duty frees at least one hour before takeoff so that there is time for them to be delivered to your departure gate.

Note
Important changes that will benefit the EC traveller come into effect on the 1st January 1993. For more information on Duty Paid and Duty Free allowances ring Customs and Excise on 071-620 1313.

o *General*

462 Buy sun hats, beach bags and some of your clothes when you get to your destination. They will most likely be cheaper. It pays to do a bit of research about bargains at your holiday resort before you shop and pack. Sunglasses are cheaper in Cyprus for example.

463 When buying souvenirs, avoid shops in busy tourist locations. You will often find better quality, cheaper souvenirs in out of the way places and quiet backstreets.

See also 222, 265, 338 and 339.

Entertainment

Theatres

464 If you're prepared to queue at the Leicester Square Ticket Booth, London WC2, you can get theatre tickets for half the usual price plus a small fee (payment by cash only). They are available from 12 noon for matinées and between 2.30 and 6.30 pm for evening performances.

465 Many bars and hotels have a 'Happy Hour' with half-price drinks at a time which fits in well after matinées or prior to an evening performance.

466 Many West End theatres offer concessions to students and senior citizens. Theatre goers of retirement age can, by producing a special card, claim a reduced rate for matinée tickets where seats are available. And seats still available just before the show starts can be bought by students at a reduced price. Further information can be obtained from The Society of West End Theatre, Bedford Chambers, Covent Garden Piazza, London WC2E 8HQ. Telephone: 071-836 0971.

467 Some theatres, including the Criterion, Wyndhams, Whitehall and Piccadilly offer discounts on car parking for those who drive into London and use NCP car parks. A parking space is reserved for your car at the time you book your ticket, and on presentation of a voucher from the theatre, the parking charge is reduced. Write to the Society of West End Theatre *(see 466)* for information on this and other cost effective ways of getting the best from London's theatreland.

468 In general, ticket agencies can charge what booking fee they like. It may be hefty or it may be nothing at all and it pays to ask before you buy tickets through them. It's often cheaper to ring the theatre direct than to use an agency. You will have to quote your credit card number, and the tickets will be sent to you or you will have to pick them up before the performance. Some theatre box offices now make a small charge for phone bookings, so ask first.

See also 231.

General

469 Keep a file of information on free entertainment. Ask your local Tourist Authority what's on, consult the local papers and pick up leaflets. Family membership of the zoological or other societies can mean cheaper entry and badges and posters etc.

470 There are toy libraries which work on the same principle as book and music libraries. If you don't already know of one in your area send a stamped addressed envelope to Play Matters, 68 Churchway, London NW1 1LT, or telephone 071-387 9592.

Gardens, Plants and Flowers

In the Garden

471 Beware of gardeners who charge an hourly rate and spin out the work when you're not around. It's often best to agree on a fixed rate for all jobs like grass cutting, hedge trimming, pruning, weeding etc. It's then in the interests of the person you employ to work quickly and efficiently.

472 Exchanging plants and seeds with a friend or as part of a group is the cheapest way to get variety. Propagating from cuttings is easy and leftover seeds can be kept in a cool pantry in a labelled, airtight container until the conditions are right for planting. They will deteriorate in stuffy garden sheds and warm kitchens but in the salad compartment of the fridge will survive in peak condition for up to 3 months.

473 If you would like to grow your own food but haven't the space, why not pay the modest sum required to rent an allotment? You'll get a tremendous return in food for the freezer, cupboards full of pickles and jams and even fresh flowers for you and friends at a fraction of the shop price. Because it's both excellent recreation and socially agreeable in the company of other keen gardeners, as well as a way to save loadsa money, there are long waiting lists in certain areas. But you can do no better than to seek advice from The National Association of Allotment and Leisure Gardeners Ltd, Hunters Road, Corby, Northants NN17 1JE. Telephone: (0536) 66576. There are over 1,500 societies around Britain, and membership enables you to cash in on bulk buys and special offers on good quality implements and sundries.

474 You can often save huge amounts of money by knowing your legal rights. A common dispute concerns trees which overhang boundaries. If a neighbour complains that branches of your trees hang over or intrude into his garden, you may want to be helpful by having them removed, but you have no legal obligation to do so. If your neighbour decides to cut them off – which he is legally able to – they are still yours and should be returned to you. Wandering roots are more difficult to deal with. If they cause any damage to a neighbour's walls or foundations you are responsible, so have potential problem roots seen to as soon as you can.

475 When buying a wheelbarrow you'll find cheaper and tougher models at builders' merchants than at garden centres and DIY stores. Builders' wheelbarrows are designed to withstand rough ground and heavy loads of rubble and cement, unlike the flimsy and often unstable wheelbarrows displayed at garden centres.

476 Where water is scarce or metered, invest in a timer tap to turn a sprinkler off automatically when the job is done. In dry spells, the recommended weekly dosage is 25 litres of water per sq metre (or 5 gallons per sq yard) to maintain a healthy lawn. Only buy new plants in autumn when they'll need less water to become established, and declare constant war on weeds as they use up precious water supplies. Also, don't dig soil which is over dry or you'll bring the damper, lower layer to the surface, causing it to dry out.

477 There is a good argument for controlling garden pests without chemical aids, leaving nature to strike a balance with the use of predators. Contact Natural Pest Control, Watermead Road, Yapton, Barnham, Bognor, Sussex PO22 0BQ. Telephone: (0243) 553250 for further information and supplies.

478 Gravel is great for smothering weeds and making a small area seem neater and larger. Buy it from builders' merchants rather than garden centres and DIY stores, especially when you need a considerable quantity. For the biggest savings buy in bulk and share with a neighbour if you can't use it all. As a shopping guide, one tonne of gravel will cover about 18 square yards (15sq m), giving a depth of 2 inches (5cm). Beware of putting limestone chippings near plants which need acid soil (rhododendrons and azaleas for example) as it could kill them.

479 Buying paving slabs is easy enough but it pays to compare prices between garden centres, DIY stores and builders' merchants. The smaller the slabs, the longer it will take to lay them and the more weeds will eventually poke up unless they are cemented together when laid.

○ **Grass and lawns**

480 Professional groundsmen who have weedfree well manicured lawns owe it to the purchase of the best lawn seeds and diligent aftercare. Grass seed available from garden centres and other consumer outlets is often well past its sell-by date although this may not be obvious. If you can buy in quantity (25kg or more) you will get the best buys and superior quality using advice given in *Turfgrass Seed*, an inexpensive leaflet available from The Sports Turf Research Institute, Bingley, West Yorkshire BD16 1AV. Telephone: (0274) 565131.

481 To keep a lawn in top condition scarify it regularly making small punctures or incisions in the top soil to aerate the earth and assist drainage. An electric lawnraker is the best tool for this job but instead of buying one set aside a day in September or October and hire one. If you have a large area of grass ask your local hire shop for a petrol powered model.

See also 68-70.

482   A good well maintained mower is essential for any garden with a lawn, but because it's a substantial outlay it must be the right type for the job. For example a lightweight electric mower won't cope with bumps and rough grass. For this you'd need a small petrol rotary mower. When shopping for a new mower or scouring the for sale ads for reconditioned bargains, bear the following guidelines in mind:
Small lawns (less than 60sq yards/50sq m) – an electric mower with a cutting width of (10-12 inches 25-30cm).
Medium lawns (60-300sq yards/50-250sq m) – a petrol mower with a cutting width of (12-14 inches 30-35cm).
Large lawns (over 300sq yards/250sq m) – a self-propelled mower with grass collector and a cutting width of (14-16 inches 35-40cm).

483   Rather than buy an extra mower for a grassy bank do away with the hassle, expense and potential dangers by digging it up and laying ground plants and spring bulbs for a low mainte-nance all year round display. Or sow a mix of wild flower seeds and naturalised bulbs and let the grass gow grow wild, à la country hedgerow.

484   The *Gardening From Which?* magazine, and their action pack called *Take The Hard Work Out of Gardening* are wise purchases for anyone creating a new garden from old or seeking to run an existing one more efficiently and econom-ically. Both publications are available from the Consumers' Association, 2 Marylebone Road, London NW1 4DX.

Houseplants

485   Rainwater is the cheapest and kindest tonic of all for flowers and plants, so a water butt can prove a wise investment. Where it is necessary to use tap water, a dash of vinegar will act as a water softener. Cooled boiled water from the kettle and fizzy mineral water gone flat are free from impurities and well worth saving for plants.

486 With even the palest of green fingers you can fill a house with prolific growing houseplants. Perfect plants for the novice include the spider plant (*Clorophytum*), wandering jew (*Tradescantia*), mother-in-law's tongue (*Sansevieria*) and grape ivy (*Rhoicissus*). What's more all these plants are easy to propagate from healthy mother specimens. Spider plant shoots can be pegged down into adjoining small pots of compost until they take root when they can be detached from the parent plant. Mother-in-law's tongue chops up in pieces for easy propagation, and grape ivy and wandering jew cuttings can be taken just below a leaf joint and placed in a brown medicine bottle of water until they sprout roots.

487 Plant food is necessary for keeping plants healthy but there are cheaper alternatives to the bought variety. A few drops of castor oil fed to the compost every 6 weeks will make foliage plants (ferns in particular) greener. Never throw away the cooled water from boiled eggs as the calcium-rich water will be enormously appreciated by African violets. All plants will be grateful for leftover tea, beer and wine diluted with tepid boiled water.

488 When buying houseplants in winter avoid any which have been sitting outside on pavements or in a draughty doorway. They may appear all right at the time of purchase, but the ill treatment will have shortened the life span of the plant. Also make sure that there are no roots popping out of drainage holes in the pot, as this indicates a 'root bound' plant. Faded labels on a plant are a sure sign that it is past its sell-by date. Mottled or yellow leaves and brown tips are other obvious signs of neglect. Once satisfied with your purchase have it wrapped in stout brown paper to protect it from the elements until you get it home.

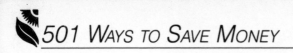

Sending Flowers

489 There is a limit to how cheaply you can send flowers. The usual way is to find a Teleflorist or Interflora member, possibly from the Yellow Pages, and place the order over the telephone or in person. The order is then passed on to a florist near the address of the recipient who will make up the order with whatever they have in stock to the chosen value, unless they have been given specific instructions otherwise. Most florists will make up from their freshest flowers, but the system allows the unscrupulous few to get rid of any which are close to fading (*see 491*). Be specific about how many and the type of flowers you want, choosing only flowers in season. Roses, for example, are abundant and comparatively cheap in summer but in winter they are not only dearer but of inferior quality. You might do considerably better by finding out the number of the floral delivery service nearest to the recipient and telephoning them yourself (*see 59*). You should save on any telephone surcharges and, not least will establish a personal rapport with the arranger.

490 When you send flowers abroad, it pays to leave the choice to the florist delivering them as you cannot possibly know what seasonal stocks they carry. Where possible, place your order weeks in advance so that it has time to go by letter, so saving expensive telephone and telex/fax charges.

491 An awkward situation can arise where flowers received in a gift are poor quality and the service has been poor (i.e. delivered later than the promised date). If you feel a refund is in order you can complain to the following addresses if the florist concerned is displaying either sign.

Interflora,
Interflora House,
Watergate,
Sleaford,
Lincolnshire
NG34 7TB
Telephone: (0529) 304141

British Teleflower
Service Ltd,
146 Bournemouth Road,
Chandlers Ford,
East Leigh,
Hampshire SO5 37B.
Telephone: (0703) 265109

Pets

Veterinary Care

492 Vets bills can dramatically inflate the cost of keeping a pet, so consider carefully taking out an insurance policy to cover veterinary fees. Treatment for even the smallest animal can cost a fortune. Your vet should be able to advise you and may have useful leaflets on the subject.

493 Lack of money can never be the excuse to neglect a pet which needs veterinary care. Contact local branches of animal welfare societies such as The Blue Cross or The People's Dispensary For Sick Animals (both listed in Yellow Pages). Although they will give free treatment, they are of course grateful for any donation. If transport is a problem they might be able to arrange this too.

494 Recently when I offered to help my hard pressed vet man his reception on a temporary basis, he waived my next bill because I hadn't accepted money. You might ask if there's any part time work you can do in exchange for pet care.

Buying Dogs and Cats

495 The most expensive way to buy a dog is from a pet shop or breeder. Unless you particularly want a puppy, why not adopt an animal who has been abandoned or neglected in a previous home? For pedigree dogs, get hold of a copy of the Dog Rescue Directory from The Kennel Club, 1 Clarges Street, London W1Y 8AB. Telephone: 071-493 6651.

496 A mongrel is hard to beat for character and temperament, and what's more they tend to have an increased resistance to some of the illnesses which plague their pedigree chums. To find a puppy of this type contact local animal welfare societies (see Yellow Pages), or Battersea Dogs Home, London.

497 Cats and kittens can be found at animal sanctuaries and are generally free to good homes, although a small donation is always well received. Also they are often advertised on notice boards at vets and animal food supply shops. Remember that a tom is easy to castrate when young, while females require a more expensive operation if they are to be speyed and save you the expense and misery of unwanted kittens.

Pet Care

498   Charity shops and jumble sales are the places to find second-hand blankets which make cheap bedding for dogs and cats. Fleecy underblankets are ideal too, and they wash brilliantly. Look out for them in the January sales.

499   Repel fleas from animals' skin by putting crushed Brewers' yeast tablets in your pet's food. Their pores will then give off an odour which will keep fleas away. Rubbing over fur with vinegar or eucalyptus oil will also deter fleas from making their home there.

500   Bicarbonate of soda makes a cheap alternative to pricey pet grooming products. It makes a good dry shampoo for dogs that also acts as a deodorant. And a rub over a dog or cat's teeth with bicarbonate of soda on a damp cloth is the answer to a pet's bad breath.

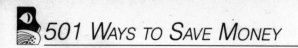

501 For older pets that are becoming stiff in the joints, a drop to a teaspoon of olive oil (depending on the size) added to their food each day seems to bring relief and delay the effects of crippling rheumatism. Olive oil may seem expensive, but not when compared to the cost of veterinary treatment. Vegetable oil will do a reasonable job of lubricating joints, and cod liver oil is highly beneficial, but dearest of all.